The Layman's Guide to Computers, the Internet, and Everything

Ian Manning

Contents

2

1 Introduction

Many people now use information technology more than they ever imagined they would, both at home and at work, but most people know very little about it. Do you harbour a nagging curiosity about how it all works?

There was a time, not too long ago, when the only visible sign of IT in the average household was an ugly beige computer and screen in the corner of a spare bedroom, and even then this was strictly for enthusiasts or IT professionals. Nowadays the sight of a laptop or tablet computer on the sofa in the lounge is suddenly not so unusual. Increasingly we are also seeing people pulling smartphones out of their pockets, to check for incoming text messages or to keep in touch with their social network of choice. Even the internals of modern TV sets now have more in common with computer s than the old boxes of valves and cathode ray tubes of 30 years ago.

To some, IT is something to be endured or even avoided if possible. If that's you, then I think it's safe to say that this book isn't for you. There are others, however, who harbour a nagging curiosity about how it all works. If that's you, then keep reading....

I recently retired from a career in Information Technology (or "data processing" as it was known when I started my career). In recent years I, like many of my peers, have been regularly pounced upon in social gatherings to help someone with an ongoing problem that they've got with their computer. On many of those occasions it occurred to me that, with just a little more insight into their technology, many people may actually be surprisingly well-equipped to resolve problems without help from an "expert".

I have also been surprised at how "tech-savvy" some of my non-technical friends have become in the last few years. When I hear them casually talking about IP addresses and reseting their wi-fi routers I wonder when this type of talk started leaking into mainstream parlance.

So why would you want to read this book? Maybe you're a closet geek, and have always secretly wanted to know more about the mysterious world of bits, bytes and wi-fi. More likely, you'd feel more comfortable knowing a little more about the technology that you use in your daily life so that you'd be better able to deal with it when it doesn't all work as it should.

Sometimes a problem can be resolved very effectively without actually needing to know why the solution worked. Remember the days of whacking the side of a TV set to sort out a dodgy picture? How many of us know why that worked? Incidentally, if you're having problems with your computer I strongly recommend that you don't try the same approach – reading some of the sections in this book will help you to understand why!

In most cases however finding a solution is much easier if you have a little background knowledge. A good analogy is the level of knowledge that most drivers have when it comes to maintaining their car. It's pretty widely accepted that it's a really good idea to keep a car well supplied with oil, water and fuel. Most drivers know that their engines need oil to keep them lubricated, and that their engines would eventually seize up without it. Likewise, they know that engines like to have water circulating around them to keep them cool. And as for fuel, well…. This basic level of knowledge can guide us when we have problems. So if our car overheats the first place we look is the radiator. Likewise if we see an oil pressure warning light on the dashboard we have an idea of the potential consequences of ignoring it.

Applying the analogy to technology –would you know where to start looking if your computer suddenly started to run really slowly? How about if you were suddenly unable to access the internet? Hopefully by reading this book you'll give yourself the confidence to start diagnosing some of your own technology problems.

The aims of this book are twofold. Firstly, it aims to satisfy the curiosity of those who would like to know more about some of the technology that they use every day. Apart from general interest, a better understanding of the underlying technology can help you to make the best of what it's capable of. It can also set expectations for when you might expect to encounter problems or limitations.

The second aim is to arm people with essential information which might help them to resolve or even avert a major problem with their technology. Even if you're unable to fix a problem, sometimes having a better understanding of the likely causes can help you to work around it, or at least to avoid making the problem worse.

One of the biggest challenges when tacking this sort of subject matter is not overwhelming the reader with the use of language which is native to the technology geek. What I've tried to do is introduce the terminology underpinning some of the key technologies, but in doing so attempt to keep the explanations as straightforward as possible. Hopefully I've managed to find a balance which de-mystifies the geek-speak but doesn't leave your head spinning.

Finally, I should make it clear that much of the content covering home computer hardware is biased towards Personal Computer (PC) rather than Apple Mac hardware. The main reason for this is that the vast majority of readers are more likely to be using a PC than a Mac. Apologies to any Apple Mac devotees who may feel aggrieved by this!

2 Anatomy of a Computer

In choosing an opening chapter for a book about information technology where else to start but with the personal computer? These have been around in various forms since the 1980s, but only with the advent of broadband technology in the 21st century did they become truly ubiquitous in modern homes.

This chapter describes the main components of a typical desktop PC. By the end of this chapter you should be able to open up your own PC and identify the components described here. The more adventurous amongst you may even have the confidence to replace some of these components.

Motherboard

Let's start with the backbone of every PC – the motherboard. This is a large circuit board which occupies most of the internal dimensions of your PC case. In many cases you won't notice it because it will be buried beneath cables and other components.

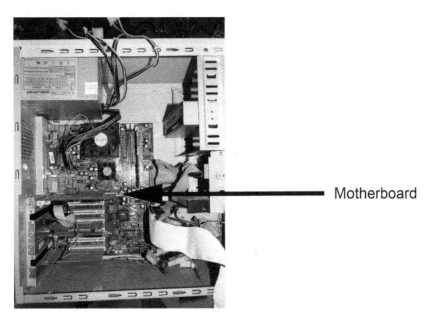

Motherboard

Figure 1 Motherboard

The motherboard performs the essential role of connecting all of the other components together. In simple terms, all of the major components of the computer are connected to the motherboard in some way, if not soldered directly onto it.

If you look at the motherboard you will usually see sockets and connectors for the followings types of components, each of which are described later in this chapter:

- Processor

- Power supply

- Disk drives

- Memory (RAM)

- USB devices

- Expansion cards.

Battery and CMOS

The motherboard will also have a small silver button-style battery sitting in a socket on the board – usually about 2cm in diameter. This provides a small amount of power to a special type of computer memory chip connected to the motherboard called CMOS (Complementary Metal Oxide Semiconductor). This memory chip is responsible for remembering a number of system settings, including the current date and time. The battery usually keeps going for a number of years before it needs replacing. If it does lose its charge one of the first things you may notice is that the date and time on your computer will no longer be correct – it will usually be reset to a base date/time like 00:00am on January 1st 1900. You will also notice that the computer "forgets" some of the details regarding the other components that are connected to it – e.g. disk drives or DVD drives.

CMOS Battery

Figure 2: CMOS Battery

So why does the motherboard require a battery if the computer is plugged into the mains? Because CMOS memory chips can only remember things for as long as they have power connected to them. When the power to the computer is switched off the contents of the CMOS memory would otherwise be lost. The battery ensures that there is a constant supply of power to these chips, even when the computer is powered off.

Processor

The most expensive component connected to any motherboard is usually the processor, sometimes called the Central Processing Unit or CPU. This is the brains of the computer. This is a small square silicon chip, less than 4cm wide. The CPU sits in a socket on the motherboard, and is usually obscured by a fan which sits directly on top of it - modern CPU's generate alot of heat, and can be damaged quite quickly if they are not kept cool.

The CPU is truly a marvel of modern science. In simple terms it processes any series of instructions or performs any calculations that it is asked to perform. This can be anything from simple arithmetic to complex decoding of computer video formats. The full story is much more impressive however, and could merit an entire publication in itself.

At any point in time the CPU is probably dealing with a long list of requests from a number of different sources. For example, the user could be watching a video while, in the background, the system is performing a check for viruses. Those two operations alone would generate millions of individual tasks for the CPU to perform.

Let's consider the playback of the video for a moment. A video consists of a series of still images (frames), played back in sequence to give the effect of motion. Every frame of the video consists of maybe a million or more individual coloured dots (pixels) which need to be displayed on the screen. The CPU needs to work out how and where to display every pixel on the screen. It needs to consider not just where to display the pixel, but also other things like the colour and level of brightness required for each. For every second of the video there could be 25-30 different frames, each containing more than a million pixels, so the CPU may need to handle the display of 25 million pixels every second.

Figure 3: CPU

Before it thinks about doing this, the CPU needs to read information about the video from the media file that the user is playing back (for example a movie that has been downloaded from the internet), and translate the contents of the file into a set of instructions for displaying the pixels. This file will probably have been compressed to keep it small (this is explained further in the chapter on Multimedia), so the CPU will first need to apply an algorithm to decompress it before it can make sense of it.

From the above (which is actually a simplification of what really happens), you can begin to get an idea of the sheer scale of the workload expected of the CPU. If it were to carry out each of these tasks one after the other, waiting for one to complete before it started the next, it probably wouldn't be able to complete all of its tasks quickly enough. If this was true, and the computer was playing a video file, then the playback would be very slow and jerky, because the processor wouldn't be able to display the pixels quickly enough.

To avoid this situation, the CPU gives itself a performance boost by carrying out lots of tasks at the same time. While this is great in theory, in practise this makes everything alot more complicated. For example, it might decide to start processing several frames of a video at the same time. Some of the frames might be easier to process than others, so it will finish processing these ones first. The problem is that the "easy" frames might need to appear later in the video than the "complicated" frames, so it will need to wait until the complicated frames have been processed before it can display the easy frames. So as well as working through all of the tasks in the queue, and performing lots of tasks at the same time, the CPU also has to be aware of which ones need to wait for others to complete first.

This is just a small taste of just how clever the CPU needs to be, but will hopefully give you an idea of why it needs that fan to keep it cool!

Power supply

The next important component connected to the motherboard is the power supply. This is usually the easiest to spot, as it will have a power lead trailing from it!

Figure 4: Power Supply

The power supply is encased in a metal housing with an embedded cooling fan, and will have an array of connector cables trailing from it. One of these cables will be plugged directly into the motherboard – this provides power to the motherboard itself. Some or all of the remaining cables will be connected to components installed in the computer – e.g. disk drives, CD or DVD drives or cooling fans attached to the computer case.

Hard disk drives and Memory

Which brings us nicely onto disk drives. Many of you will be familiar with the concept of a disk drive, sometimes known as a "hard" disk drive (mainly to differentiate it from the "floppy" disks which used to be a feature of home computers until quite recently).

A hard disk drive is an example of another type of *memory* used by a computer (we have already discussed CMOS memory). Computers use memory for storing various types of content:

- User data - this is data which you have created or acquired yourself – e.g. word processing documents, spreadsheets, digital photos, music, video files, etc.

- Programs – these are sets of instructions (also known as applications) which are installed on your computer. Examples might be word processors, spreadsheet programs or music players.

- System data – these are files which are essential for the running of the computer. These include the files required by the operating system, which is described in a later chapter.

Memory in a computer can be classified as either *primary* or *secondary* memory. Primary memory is used for storing relatively small amounts of data which need to be accessed at high speed, and is usually based on silicon chips. Primary memory itself may fall into two categories: *volatile* memory requires power in order to retain its contents, whereas *non-volatile* memory does not. CMOS is a good example of volatile memory – this is why it requires a battery to retain its contents.

Secondary memory is used for storing much larger volumes of data, but it is much slower to access. A hard disk is a good example of secondary memory.

Figure 5: Hard Disk Drive

Hard disk drives are roughly the size and shape of a small paperback book, and are mounted in a rack in the computer case. A computer will usually have at least one hard disk drive installed, but may have several – although typically no more than 3 or 4. Each hard disk will have two cables connected to it:

- A power cable from the power supply

- A data cable, connected to the motherboard.

It's worth knowing a little about hard disk drives, as you'll probably have information stored on them which you really wouldn't want to lose.

The first thing to know is that they are extremely sophisticated, but quite fragile pieces of engineering. Inside a hard disk drive you will find one or more rotating disks (often referred to as "platters"). If there is more than one disk, the disks are arranged in a stack, one above the other. Each disk is covered with magnetic material, much like the magnetic material found in old music cassette tapes. Data is read from the disks, or written to them, by magnetic "heads". These heads are mounted on a moving arm, with each head floating very close to the surface of the disk(s). It is important that the heads do not actually make physical contact with the disks, as this could damage the disk irreparably, and cause the loss of the data stored on the disk. If there is significant physical impact to the hard disk drive this could cause one or more of the heads to "crash" into a disk – for this reason it is important that the drive is not accidentally knocked while it is working.

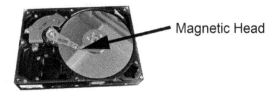
Magnetic Head

Figure 6: Inside a Hard Disk Drive

To help avoid the heads crashing into the disk platters, the arm on which the heads are mounted is designed to automatically "park" the heads in a safe location away from the disks whenever the hard disk drive is powered down or not otherwise in use.

The data stored on hard disks is very densely populated – alot of information is packed into tiny amounts of space on the magnetic surface of the platters. In general, the higher the capacity of the hard disk, the more densely the data is packed. The nature of this technology means that sometimes the data is not always written or read 100% accurately, as it is squeezed into such a small amount of space. Because of this, disk drives use error-correction software to make sense of data when it has trouble reading it. This software works by guessing the content of missing data, based on the context of the surrounding "good" data. This is surprisingly effective, but can slow down the process of reading data from the drive.

In addition to the problems caused by the dense population of the data on the drives, the magnetic surface of the disks can also develop flaws which prevent the safe storage of data on certain areas of the disk. In fact pretty much all hard disk drives have a number of "bad sectors" which have been identified during the manufacturing process. The disk drives maintain a list of bad sectors, and avoid the use of these sectors for storing data. As and when new defects develop over time the hard disk drive tries to move data from the bad sectors to "good" sectors of the disk if it can, but eventually drives will degrade to the point where they are no longer usable. This is why it is really important to keep a backup copy of **all** of your important files – as one day the passing of time will almost certainly make them impossible to read.

Solid State Disks

One of the main drawbacks of hard disk technology is that it is largely mechanical – it relies on spinning disks, and an arm which needs to move around the disks very quickly so that the heads can read or write data magnetically on the correct part of the disk. While this all happens very quickly, it is actually very slow compared to the electronic workings of primary memory. To give you an idea, some types of data access can be 100,000 times quicker with primary memory compared to hard disk drives. Because of this, a new type of disk drive has emerged which attempts to combine the performance of primary memory with the capacity of hard disk drives. These are called solid-state disks (or SSD's).

From the outside, SSD's look identical to hard disk drives, but on the inside they are completely different. Instead of spinning disks and a mechanical arm you will find only electronic circuitry similar to that used for primary memory. They contain no moving mechanical parts, so can withstand the sorts of knocks that would ruin a hard disk drive. The memory used is also non-volatile, so retains its contents when no power is connected to it. SSD's also consume less power than hard disk drives.

SSD's can be up to 10 times faster than hard disk drives, but are much more expensive for similar storage capacity. SSD's are also not currently available in the largest capacities currently offered by hard disk drives. Despite this, many believe that SSD's are the way of the future, and their price is falling rapidly as they become more popular.

Optical Media

Another popular type of secondary memory is optical media. Examples of optical media are CDs, DVDs and Blu-Ray disks. These are the same types of disks that are used in home entertainment equipment, and have become a popular way of storing data for use on computers.

Your computer will almost certainly have some sort of device or "drive" for reading (and maybe writing) some form of optical media. The most popular device on most modern computers is a DVD drive. A DVD drive, in common with other optical drives on a computer, looks like a miniature version of a CD player. It is mounted on the front of the computer, and will have either a slot or a slide-out tray for inserting disks.

If you look at the back of an optical drive you will see it is connected to the computer in the same way as a hard disk drive – one cable going to the power supply and a separate data cable connected to the motherboard.

Optical media uses laser technology to "burn" patterns onto the surface of a disk. These patterns are used to represent data. Most optical media can only be "burned" once – i.e. once a pattern has been written to the disk it cannot be altered. However there are also re-writable types of optical media, which can be burned multiple times, so you can erase and re-use the disks if you choose.

Optical media disks are relatively cheap to purchase, but have a much lower storage capacity than hard disk drives. To give you an idea, Blu-Ray disks have the highest capacity of the popular types of optical media. Most computers have a hard disk drive which is more than 5 times the capacity of the largest Blu-Ray disk.

Optical disks are a popular way of making permanent backup copies of valuable files. For example, many people copy their digital photos from their computer to DVDs and store them in a folder for safe-keeping. They are also a good way of sharing content with friends.

RAM

The last important type of memory that you should be aware of is RAM (Random Access Memory). This is primary memory, and usually takes the form of up to four long thin computer chips which are plugged into the motherboard, perpendicular to the motherboard.

RAM Slots

Figure 7: RAM Memory

RAM is volatile memory (so loses its contents when the computer is switched off). It is in constant use by the computer when it is running. RAM is an extremely fast form of memory, and is used as a sort of high-speed scratchpad area by the computer. When the computer is executing instructions (e.g. a program) it will first load the program, or part of it, into RAM. It will also load any data required by that program into RAM. For example, if you are writing a document using a word processor it will load both the word processor program and the document that you are working on (or at least parts of each) into RAM. A copy of both the program and the document will also exist on the hard disk drive, but the hard disk drive is much too slow to keep up with the processor. While you are using the word processor the CPU is constantly reading program instructions from RAM, as well as reading and writing the contents of your document in RAM. When you save the document, its contents are copied from RAM back onto the hard disk drive.

Because RAM is relatively expensive most computers have a limited amount of it installed. For example, the main hard disk in a computer would usually be at least 100 times larger than the amount of RAM installed in the computer. For this reason a computer can quite quickly "run out" of RAM. For example if you are editing a very large word processing document this may be occupying a large chunk of the available RAM. The word processing program will be occupying another large chunk. The system itself requires a fair amount of RAM to support a variety of processes that it needs to run in the background (these processes will be largely invisible to the user, but are essential to the running of the computer). When the computer starts to run out of RAM it needs to take some measures which can seriously slow things down for the user – this will be explained in the next chapter.

Bits and Bytes

So far we've discussed several different types of memory, but we haven't talked about the basic units that are used to measure the size of data.

As many of you will probably know, data used in computing is stored in binary format. The smallest unit of data is a bit – a tiny number which can only have a value of zero or one. The next smallest unit is a byte, which is usually a collection of 8 bits. The mathematicians among you will know that if you have a collection of 8 bits, each having one of two possible values, then the number of permutations of values for a collection of 8 bits is 256 (i.e. 2 to the power 8). To put it in another way, a byte may have any one of 256 different values.

A byte can be used to express many different types of information. In its simplest form, it can represent any number from 1 to 256. Alternatively, it could be used to express a letter of the alphabet – since there are only 26 letters in the alphabet this can be done with 230 permutations to spare!

A number of different coding systems exist to define possible interpretations of the value of a byte. One popular coding system is called ASCII (American Standard Code for Information Interchange). In this system a byte is used to represent a character from an extended range of characters, including:

- upper and lower case variations of the letters of the alphabet

- numbers from 0 to 9

- "special" characters such as commas, question marks and other punctuation characters.

So for example in the ASCII coding system if a byte has a value of 65 then it represents a capital "A". A value of 66 represents a capital "B". A value of 97 represents a lower case "a", while 98 represents a lower case "b". A value of 63 represents a question mark. A value of 32 is a space character.

So if you wanted to represent the phrase "Who Are You?" using the ASCII coding system you would need 12 bytes (one for each character, if you include the spaces between words) with values as below:

Character	W	h	o		A	r	e		Y	o	u	?
Byte Value	87	104	111	32	65	114	101	32	89	111	117	63

Figure 8:ASCII example

Extrapolating the above example: if you had a page of text containing 600 words, with an average of 6 letters in each word, plus 600 spaces or punctuation characters between words, you would need 4,200 bytes to store that page if you used the ASCII coding system. So a book of 500 pages would require 2,100,000 bytes.

Thankfully, values like this can be expressed more simply in terms of kilobytes, megabytes, gigabytes and terabytes, etc. Here's how it all adds up:

- 1 kilobyte (kB) = 1,024 bytes

- 1 megabyte (MB) = 1,024 kilobytes

- 1 gigabyte (GB) = 1,024 megabytes

- 1 terabyte (TB) = 1,024 gigabytes

- 1 petabyte (PB) = 1,024 gigabytes

So in the example above, our 500-page book could be stored in a little over 2 megabytes (MB) if the ASCII coding system was used.

Computers are of course used to store many other types of file – for example digital photos, music and video files. This topic is covered later in this book, but to give you an idea how many bytes each of these media might require:

- A DVD can store a little over 4 gigabytes

- A CD can store approximately 650 megabytes

- An mp3 music track is usually 3-5 megabytes

- A 1-megapixel digital photo is around 1 megabyte.

So if your digital photo files were 1 MB each, then you could fit just over 4,000 photos onto a DVD.

A modern computer usually has between 2 and 8 gigabytes of RAM installed, whereas the hard disk drive is usually a minimum of 250 gigabytes.

Expansion slots

Motherboards usually have a number of expansion slots (also called expansion ports) which can be used to add new capabilities to your computer. There may be up to 7 of these slots in a typical computer. They are typically arranged parallel to each other, with the end of each slot adjacent to the rear of the computer.

By inserting a circuit board (often referred to as an "expansion card") into one of these slots you can do things such as:

- Improve the graphics capabilities of the computer – for example to speed up the display of complex images, or to improve performance when playing games
- Improve the audio quality of your computer when playing music or video files
- Allow new or specialist hardware devices to be connected to the computer
- Expand the memory that is connected to the computer.

Expansion slots on motherboards come in different types and sizes. There are two basic sizes: half- and full-size. Half-size slots are also called 8-bit slots because they can transfer 8 bits of data at a time between the motherboard and the expansion card. Full-size slots are sometimes called 16-bit slots.

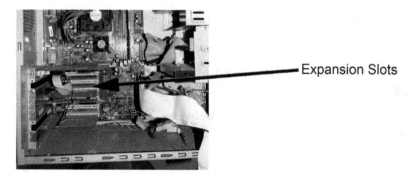

Figure 9: Expansion Slots

The different types of expansion slots/expansion cards are:

- PCI (Peripheral Component Interconnect) – this is the most common type of expansion slot found in modern computers

- PCI Express (also known as PCIe) – this is the fastest and most efficient type of expansion slot

- AGP (Accelerated Graphics Port) - this is specifically intended for use with graphics adapters – see below for more information about graphics adapters. AGP ports are becoming less popular with modern computers, as many high performance graphics adapters now use PCI Express

- ISA (Industry Standard Architecture) - this is the oldest type of expansion slot. Many modern computers may not have any ISA slots – they would be only included to allow older expansion cards to be connected to the computer.

Graphics adapter

The graphics adapter is the component which is responsible for sending output to your screen (this may also be called a graphics card, video adapter or display adapter). It generates all of the text and pictures and sends the necessary electronic signals to display them on your screen.

The graphics adapter is usually a circuit board which is inserted into one of the expansion slots on the motherboard. Some motherboards have graphics adapters built-in to them, and hence do not require a separate adapter in an expansion slot.

The work done by the graphics adapter, particularly when displaying pictures rather than text, can be extremely complex. The following are the sorts of things that need to be considered by the graphics adapter:

- Resolution – this is the number of coloured dots (pixels) which are displayed on the screen - the more pixels that are used the sharper the image appears on the screen. The resolution can be selected by the user, but will ultimately be constrained by the capabilities of your screen (monitor) – each monitor will have a maximum resolution which it is capable of displaying. An example of a popular resolution is 1024 x 768 – this means that the display will be composed of 786,432 coloured dots, arranged in 1,024 columns and 768 rows

- Colour depth – this defines the range of variation of colours that a single dot (pixel) can have. It is usually expressed as a number, this being the number of bits used to express the colour. For example a colour depth of 16 bits means that 16 bits of data are used to specify the pixel colour. This means that a pixel could be any one of 65,536 colours (i.e. 2 to the power 16)

- Refresh rate – this is how many times per second the image on the screen is redrawn. The unit of measure is hertz (Hz). A refresh rate of 60Hz means that the image on the screen is redrawn 60 times every second. The higher refresh rate is the better, but once again this will be limited by the maximum refresh rate that can be supported by your monitor. Refresh rate becomes very important when watching fast-moving images – for example when playing certain fast-paced games.

The workload of the graphics adapter increases dramatically when it needs to display 3D images. Many games now make use of fast-moving 3D imagery for example. This has led to the increased popularity of specialist 3D graphics adapters. Many of these have built-in capabilities commonly required in games such as applying textures to surfaces, or transparency effects to glass or water.

Rear panel connections

On the back of your computer you will see a variety of ports (sockets) for connecting cables. Since you may need to use some or all of these, it's worth knowing what they are for. This section describes the most commons types of connectors.

Keyboard port - this may be used to connect a keyboard to your computer. Many modern keyboards now use the USB connector instead (see below).

Mouse port - this may be used to connect a mouse to your computer. Many modern mice now use the USB connector instead (see below).

Speaker port – this is used to connect stereo speakers (or headphones) to the computer.

Microphone port – this is used to connect a microphone to the computer.

Keyboard port

Mouse port

Speaker port

Microphone port

Display port (VGA)

Display port (HDMI)

Display port (DVI)

Universal Serial Bus (USB) port

Ethernet port

Digital audio port

eSata port

Parallel port

Figure 10: Rear panel connections

Display port – this is used to connect your screen (monitor) to your computer. The graphics adapter on your computer will have one of these connectors either built into it or connected to it via a cable. There are several different types of display connector:

- VGA (Video Graphics Array) – this is the oldest and most common type of connector. There is also a variant of this called SVGA (Super Video Graphics Array)

- DVI (Digital Visual Interface) – this is a more recent type of connector, and is capable of handling more types of video signals than the VGA connector

- HDMI (High Definition Multimedia Interface) – this connector can carry sound as well as high-definition video signals. HDMI connectors are also a popular way of connecting high definition televisions and projectors to other components such as DVD or Blu-Ray players.

Universal Serial Bus (USB) ports – these are a multi-purpose connector which can be used to connect a variety of different components to your computer – e.g. keyboards, mice, printers, scanners, cameras, external hard disk drives, memory sticks, smartphones. This type of connector was first introduced in the 1990s, and replaced earlier types of connectors called parallel interfaces (used mainly for printers) and serial interfaces. As well as allowing connected devices to share data with your computer, the USB connector can also supply power to the connected device, so it can be a convenient way of charging a device. If used for this purpose it's worth knowing that a dedicated USB charging device which plugs directly into the mains will almost certainly charge your device more quickly, as the USB connectors on a computer are usually designed to supply a smaller electrical charging current than a dedicated power supply.

Ethernet port – this is used to connect your computer to a network. In simple home setups this is often used to connect the computer to a broadband internet router.

Digital audio port – these are used to connect your computer to a hi-fi audio system using high quality digital signals.

eSata port – these are used to connect external hard disk drives to your computer.

Parallel port – this is an older style connection, usually used to connect your computer to a printer. On most modern computers the parallel port has been superseded by USB ports.

Laptops

So far this chapter has focused on the components of a desktop computer. You will not be surprised to hear that a laptop contains most of the same components. The layout and physical appearance will be very different however, due to the need to condense all of the components into a much smaller space.

The most obvious difference is that the screen and keyboard are integrated with the laptop case, and are usually connected to the motherboard using a flat ribbon-style cable. The motherboard in a laptop is also much smaller than the one in a desktop computer, and is more difficult to access.

Laptop motherboards will not have the range of expansion slots that can be found on most desktops. Instead, a laptop will often have a slot for an expansion card which is roughly the size of a credit card (although not as thin as a credit card). On a modern laptop this expansion slot will be what is known as an ExpressCard interface. In older laptops this would have been a different type of slot called a PC Card slot (also known as PCMCIA). Graphics adapters tend to be integrated into the motherboard in a laptop.

Most laptops will have at least one USB connector, as well as an Ethernet connector and a headphone/speaker connector.

The hard disk drive in a laptop will be similar to that in a desktop, but will be physically smaller – a desktop hard disk drive will usually be 3.5 inches wide, whereas a laptop drive will be 2.5 inches wide. The power and data connectors at the back of the disk drive will be virtually identical however. In fact a 2.5 inch drive from a laptop can usually be plugged directly into a desktop computer.

The use of SSD's (solid state drives) in laptops is becoming increasingly popular as an alternative to hard disk drives. As well as the performance benefits, SSD's also tend to consume less power than hard disk drives, which means that the laptop's battery will last longer. Also, the fact that there are no moving mechanical parts in an SSD means that it is far more suited to the travelling lifestyle of a laptop. It means that the laptop is far more able to survive the bumps and knocks of life on the road.

Upgrade options are usually far more limited on a laptop than a desktop. Graphics adapters are very rarely upgradable, although in some cases there are ways to use external graphics adapters. The most easily removable/upgradable component in a laptop is usually the hard disk drive. This can typically be accessed by removing a couple of screws from the base of the laptop and removing a cover.

RAM can often be upgraded on laptops – once again this is usually accessible by removing a couple of screws and removing a cover from the base of the laptop. Because of the compressed internal layout of a laptop, RAM chips are much smaller than their equivalent in desktop computers.

The one component found on all laptops, but not desktops, is the battery. This is a relatively heavy component, and can often be removed and replaced. Where the battery is removable it can usually be identified as a long, thin slab, usually at the back of the base of the laptop.

The life of a laptop battery degrades over time. It is not uncommon for a laptop battery to last little more than 30 minutes after only a few years of use. For this reason it is always a distinct advantage to choose a laptop with a removable battery!

3 Getting Up and Running

The previous chapter described the basic components of a computer. This chapter describes what happens when you press the power button and the computer starts up. It explains the roles played by the components described in the previous chapter, and covers some basic concepts and principles about what is happening while the computer is up and running.

Powering up

So what happens when you press the power button on a computer? The answer is that a process is started that, if successful, will bring the computer to life and prepare it for use.

The startup process of a computer is often called the boot process. This is short for bootstrap, and is derived from the idea of pulling oneself up by one's bootstraps.

When you press the power button the first thing that happens is that the power supply springs into life, and starts supplying power to all of the components connected to it. The most important component at this stage is the CPU connected to the motherboard, which is responsible for starting the boot process.

The first thing that the CPU needs is a set of instructions for starting the boot process. It finds these instructions from a memory chip on the motherboard called the BIOS (Basic Input-Output System). This is a non-volatile memory chip, so the instructions are always retained even when the power is turned off.

The first instruction is called the power-on self test (POST). This does a number of things:

- Checks the BIOS chip

- Tests the CMOS and the battery, as described above

- Checks the list of hardware devices which will be required to complete the boot process, to ensure that they are working properly – e.g. the graphics adapter, secondary memory devices such as hard disk drives, and the keyboard.

If any of the above checks fail the computer will display a message on the screen, indicating the problem that it has encountered. If no problems are found then the next step is to look for an *operating system* to load.

An operating system (often abbreviated to OS) is the most important program that your computer needs to run. Without it, the computer is virtually useless. Operating systems are described in more detail in the next section, but for now it's worth knowing that you will not be able to run any other programs until the operating system has been loaded.

So how does the BIOS program know where to find the operating system? It usually looks to the CMOS chip to tell it. On most computers the operating system is stored on a hard disk drive. It can also be loaded from other places however - for example a DVD drive or even a memory stick inserted into a USB port. The CMOS chip gives the BIOS program a list of places to look for the operating system, and tells it which order to check them in (this order is called the *boot sequence*). For example, it may tell the BIOS to check the hard disk drive first, and if it doesn't find an operating system there then check the DVD drive next.

When it checks each place for an operating system the first thing it looks for is a chunk of data called the *boot record*. This will tell it where to find the beginning of the operating system program. If it cannot find a boot record on any of the places on the list then it will display a message and the boot process will come to a halt.

Once the operating system is found the BIOS copies its files into memory (RAM) so that they can be accessed more quickly, and from that point onwards the CPU uses the operating system program to finish the boot process.

The operating system will conduct its own check of how much memory is available, and will load a series of small programs called *device drivers* into memory. These are required to control hardware devices connected to the computer - e.g. the mouse, keyboard, optical drives, printers, scanners.

Once all of the device drivers are loaded the boot process is complete. At this point the user is able to start using the computer.

Operating systems

The operating system is usually the largest and most complex program you will find on a computer. It is responsible for a number of essential tasks, such as:

- Recognising input from the keyboard or mouse

- Sending output to the display (via the graphics adapter)

- Keeping track of all of the data and programs in both primary and secondary memory

- Controlling hardware connected to the computer – e.g. hard disk drives, DVD drives, printers, etc.

At any point in time there may be lots of things going on inside the computer – the operating system must ensure that they don't interfere with each other. It must also ensure that unauthorised users are prevented from accessing the system.

The operating system is the software platform on which other programs (applications) can run. Each application is written to run on top of a specific operating system. For this reason, the operating system that you choose will largely dictate which applications you will be able to run. The three most popular operating systems on home computers are Windows, Apple Mac and Linux.

The operating system acts as a buffer between programs running on the computer and the hardware connected to the computer. Many programs will run on the computer, often at the same time, and they will require access to the same pool of hardware resources. For example, most programs will want to display something on the screen, or read data from the hard disk drive, or simply use some RAM to store some data temporarily. The operating system manages the demand for these resources, and makes sure that access to the hardware is shared in a way that doesn't overload the hardware and also doesn't keep any program waiting too long for access to a hardware device.

The user interacts with the operating system using a range of commands. In early operating systems these commands were typed directly using the keyboard using a text-based interface commonly known as a "green screen". So for example if you wanted to copy a file from one place to another you would type the "COPY" command, followed by details of the file and where you wanted to copy it. If you wanted to run a program you would type the name of the program. Nowadays many modern operating systems provide a graphical interface, allowing users to issue commands to the operating system by pointing and clicking at objects on the screen using a mouse. So if you want to run a program you need only click on an icon on the screen, rather than typing the name of the program. This has become by far the most popular style of interface for home computers, although many larger computers used in corporate environments still retain a text-based interface where commands are typed directly into a "green screen" type interface. There remain a surprisingly large number of IT professionals who actually prefer to work that way!

File systems

All operating systems need a method of organising the data that they need to handle. As previously discussed, this can include user-created files as well as programs and system data.

The main method used to organise data is called a file system. Each unit of data to be managed is stored in an electronic file, and these files are grouped into folders (also called directories). Each folder may have sub-folders, which themselves may have sub-folders.

File names often consist of two parts, separated by a dot. The first part is a descriptive name and the second part describes what sort of file it is. The second part is called the file extension. For example, a simple file which contains only text information may have a file extension of txt. So an example of the name of such a file might be myfile.txt. The file extension can be used to determine what sort of program is usually used to open the file. So a file with an extension of .txt would usually be opened using a text editing program for example.

Folder names are usually prefixed by the "/" or "\" character when they are written. Typically the "\" character is used in Windows file systems, whereas the "/" character is more common in other file systems.

So if you have a folder in a Windows operating system called *myfolder* it may be written as *myfolder*. In the case of sub-folders, the "/" or "\" character is used to separate folder and sub-folder names. So if you have a sub-folder in *myfolder* called *mysubfolder* then it would be referred to as *myfolder**mysubfolder*. If your *myfile.txt* file was stored in this subfolder then you could refer to it using its full address as *myfolder\mysubfolder\myfile.txt*.

As well as files and folders, the Windows operating system also has the concept of *drive letters*. This concept dates back to the very first personal computers in the 1980s. The idea is that a computer could have a number of secondary storage devices connected to it – typically one or more diskette drives and one or more hard disk drives. Each device would have an alphabetic letter assigned to identify it, and this letter was suffixed with a colon - for example the first device might be referred to as "A:"

Historically, the letters A: and B: were reserved for diskette drives. Since many of the early personal computers did not have hard disk drives they would only have diskette drives referred to as A: (and B: where there was a second drive). When hard disk drives first started to appear they were usually assigned the letter C:. This was true even if there was no A: or B: drive, as the A: and B: drive letters were reserved just in case diskette drives were added at a later date!

The convention of a hard disk drive being assigned the letter C: has endured to the current day, even though few modern computers have diskette drives. On Windows systems this is usually the place where the operating system files are stored.

Each secondary storage device will have a file system on it. On a Windows system the folders in a file system are usually prefixed with the drive letter when referring to them. So in the previous example, if the folders concerned were located on the C: drive (i.e. the first hard disk drive) then they would be referred to as *C:\myfolder\mysubfolder*.

The top level of a file system is called the *root* folder or *root directory*. So in the example above *myfolder* is a sub-folder of the root folder on the C: drive.

Windows operating systems usually display folders and sub-folders in a graphical style:

Figure 11:Folders, sub-folders and files

In the above example, the folders and subfolders are shown on the left, and the contents of the selected subfolder (C:\myfolder\mysubfolder) are shown on the right.

In non-Windows systems the concept of drive letters does not exist. Instead, storage devices are assigned names. This is a more flexible way of organising files and folders, and is also much better suited to networked environments, which are explored in more detail in the next chapter.

Virtual Memory

We have already discussed how RAM is used when you launch a program on the computer – the program that you launch is copied from a secondary storage device (typically a hard disk drive) into RAM, where the program instructions can be accessed at the speed required by the CPU. Any data required by the program is also loaded into RAM for fast access.

We have also learnt that RAM is in relatively short supply, and that if several programs are open at the same time the computer may not have enough RAM to accommodate them all. As soon as a program is closed it should release the RAM memory that it was using, but what happens if many programs are left open and the computer runs out of RAM? The answer is that the computer starts to offload some of the RAM contents into a file in secondary memory – usually on a hard disk drive – to free up space in RAM. This process is called *paging*.

The file that the RAM contents are copied to is called the *page file*. This is also commonly known as *virtual memory*. The computer will only move *some* of the RAM contents to the page file – it will try to move only the programs and data which are not currently in use. For example, if you have several programs open in different windows it will try to identify the ones which you haven't interacted with for a while and

31

move those to the page file.

At some stage the programs that have been moved from RAM to the page file will be required again. Usually this is when you return to a program that you had previously opened, but which you had not been using for a while. When this time comes the computer needs to move the program and its data back from the page file to RAM. Depending on how much RAM is available, this may also mean that it needs to move a different program from RAM to the page file to create some space for the program that it needs to copy back.

The paging process described above can be one of the most noticeable causes of slow performance on a computer. This is because reading and writing data to/from hard disk drives is one of the slowest activities that a computer carries out. If you only run one program at a time you are unlikely to see this problem. If you often have several programs running at the same time you are more likely to see it, particularly if you have a limited amount of RAM installed on your computer.

Most computers have a small light on the front of the case which illuminates when the hard disk drive is being accessed. If you find that your computer is running extremely slowly, and that this light is staying on for long periods, then it could be that the paging process is causing the problem.

The simplest way of avoiding the paging process is to ensure that you don't run out of RAM. You can do this by limiting the number of programs that are running at the same time. Ideally you should close each program as soon as you have finished using it (this should free up the RAM that it was using) although this may not always be practical.

Managing RAM is also made more complicated by two other factors. Firstly, the operating system needs a significant amount of RAM to run itself, and will claim this when the computer starts up. Secondly, when you close some programs they may not release *all* of the RAM that they were using. This problem is referred to as a *memory leak*.

From the above you can see that having as much RAM as possible installed on your computer is a good idea if you tend to have many programs open at the same time, as this will reduce or maybe even eliminate the paging process.

4 Networks and the Internet

Up to now we have described a simple environment in which there is only one computer. As you know, we now live in a world where billions of computers can communicate with each other. They can do this through the power of *networks*.

This chapter will deal with two of the more common types of network:

- Local Area Networks – you will find these in most modern office environments and alot of home computing environments

- Wide Area Networks – the best example of a Wide Area Network is the Internet.

Local Area Networks

A local area network (LAN) is a computer network that allows computing devices in the same location to communicate with each other. For example this could be an office, a home or a school.

The technology used to connect the devices together can use cables or can be wireless. In many cases a network includes both cabled and wireless elements. Cabled connections are usually much faster than wireless connections.

Physical connections

Let's start with a simple example: we have 3 computers which all need to be connected to the same network using a cabled connection. The most popular type of cable used for this purpose is called e*thernet* cable. The two most common variants of ethernet cabling are called "Category 5" (known as Cat5 or Cat5e) and "Category 6" (known as Cat6). Both are perfectly suitable for use in this situation.

Each computer will require one ethernet cable to connect it to the network. This cable should be plugged into to the Ethernet port at the back of the computer. But where should we connect the other ends of these 3 cables? The answer is that they need to be plugged into a piece of network equipment which will connect them all together. There are three options for the equipment that you need: a *hub,* a *switch* or a *router*. These are similar-looking devices, consisting of a box with a number of sockets (ports) for connecting Ethernet cables.

Hubs, switches and routers each have different capabilities, but all share the same ability to connect several computers or other devices together into a network, using ethernet cables.

The number of ports in a hub/switch/router typically varies from 4 to 48, so the boxes can vary in size quite considerably. A 4-port switch/hub/router is usually no larger than a paperback book. All hubs/switches/routers need to be connected to a power supply.

Network addresses

When all three computers have been connected to the hub/switch/router using Ethernet cables, the next step is to give each computer an address so that they can recognise each other.

In much the same way as telephones have numbers so that they can dial each other, computers on a network need addresses so that they can communicate with each other. This address is set up using special commands in the operating system. The convention used for these addresses is defined in a standard called the Internet Protocol (IP). The address given to each computer is called an IP address. This takes the form of four numbers separated by dots: for example 192.168.1.100. Each number can be in the range 0 to 255, which means that there can be about 4.3 billion different IP addresses.

There are two ways of assigning an IP address to a computer. The first is to assign a permanent address to it which it will keep even if the computer is switched off. This is called a *static* IP address. The other way is to ask for an address to be assigned to the computer automatically whenever the computer is switched on. This is called a *dynamic* IP address.

If you want to use dynamic IP addresses then there must be a device on the same network running a program called a DHCP Server (Dynamic Host Configuration Protocol). The job of this program is to look out for new computers appearing on the network and to allocate a new IP address to each computer which has not already been allocated to another computer on the network. Dynamic IP addresses are always temporary – they will expire after a set amount of time (this could be hours or maybe days) as determined by the DHCP server. Hence the addresses are said to be "leased" from the DHCP server. At the end of this time the computer may request an extension of this lease in order to keep its IP address. If the DHCP server does not hear from the computer again after the lease has expired then it makes its IP address available to any other new computers that want to join the network. This doesn't prevent the original computer re-joining the network again in the future, but it does mean that it may not get the same IP address as before.

Dynamic IP addressing tends to be quite popular. Amongst other benefits, it takes away the need to manage duplication of IP addresses on the network – e.g. inadvertently having two computers on the network with the same IP address. The DHCP server program can run on most computers and operating systems. It is also often run on routers, which themselves have mini operating systems embedded in them.

As well as an IP address, each computer needs to have something called a *subnet mask* specified for it. Subnet masks are a way of dividing networks into smaller networks (sub-networks). If you think of an IP address as being similar to a telephone number, then you can think of a subnet mask as being similar to a country dialing code. The IP address, when combined with the subnet mask, provides a unique way of addressing a computer on a network.

A subnet mask has a similar format to an IP address – i.e. four numbers separated by dots. Every computer on a network must have the **same subnet mask** as the other computers on the same network. Common examples of subnet masks might be:

255.255.255.0

255.255.0.0

One important thing to note is that the IP addressing scheme described above (four numbers separated by dots) is due to be replaced in the near future. It will be replaced by a standard called IP version 6 (the current standard is IP version 4). The new standard will introduce much longer IP addresses, and because of this will allow a much higher number of different IP addresses to be defined.

Wireless networks

In the example above our computers were connected to the network using cables. While this is the best option from a performance perspective, it may not always be practical or convenient to run cables around the place. For this reason the use of wireless networking has become extremely popular in recent years.

The idea is that, instead of data travelling over physical cables, it travels over radio waves instead – in the same way that radio broadcasts have been transmitted to radios for the last 100 years. This method of sending computer data via radio waves is called *wi-fi*.

To network computers together in this way you need a device very similar to the hub/switch/router in the example above, but instead of having ports to connect Ethernet cables it will have a radio transmitter/receiver built into it. This device will be a *wireless router* or *wireless access point*. Computers connect to this device via radio waves instead of an Ethernet cable, so the computer will need a wireless radio receiver/transmitter in order to do this. While all modern laptops have one of these built in, desktop computers tend not to. If you want to connect a desktop computer to a wireless router/access point you can add a wireless radio receiver/transmitter to it quite easily – the most obvious way would be to buy one that connects to one of the USB ports on the computer. These devices are called wi-fi adapters.

In reality most wireless routers and access points usually have Ethernet ports built into them as well as radio equipment. There are two reasons for this. Firstly, this gives you the option of connecting computers to it via either wireless or ethernet cable. So for example you may choose to connect your desktop computer using a cable, but to use wi-fi for your laptop. Secondly, it allows the router/access point to be connected to other hubs/switches/routers on the network using an Ethernet cable.

While wi-fi offers obvious benefits in terms of convenience, there are two major drawbacks. Firstly, wi-fi networks are much slower than cabled Ethernet networks - i.e. it takes data much longer to travel over a wi-fi network than it does to travel over an Ethernet cable. Secondly, wi-fi networks are limited in the distance that they can cover. Typically they are limited to a range of about 50 feet in an indoors environment where signals need to travel through walls and ceilings.

Powerline ethernet

One of the main drawbacks of a cabled network is the inconvenience of having to run Ethernet cables over potentially long distances. While modern offices have Ethernet cabling pre-installed in walls, floors or ceilings, the same is not usually true for domestic properties. So if you want a computer in your study to connect to the same network as a computer in your spare bedroom you will either have to use a wi-fi connection or find some way of installing Ethernet cabling between the two rooms. If you choose wi-fi as the solution then you may have problems with the strength of the wi-fi radio signals if your house is large, or if there are several walls and ceilings between the wi-fi router and your computer. Thankfully, there is an alternative way of extending Ethernet cabling between different locations in a building.

The idea is that you use the electricity cables already installed in the walls, floors and ceilings of your house to carry data. This effectively turns your house's electrical wiring into Ethernet cabling. In order to do this you need to plug small devices called Powerline Ethernet Adapters into your existing electrical sockets. These adapters convert computer data into a form which can be carried over electrical wiring. Each adapter has a built-in Ethernet socket so that you can plug an Ethernet cable into it.

So if you want to connect a computer in your study to the same network as a computer in your spare bedroom you could do the following:

- Install a switch in your study (this could also be a router or a hub)

- Connect the computer in your study to the switch using an Ethernet cable (exactly as per the cabled network example above)

- Plug a Powerline Ethernet Adapter into an electrical socket in your study

- Connect the switch in your study to the Powerline Ethernet Adapter using an Ethernet cable

- Plug a Powerline Ethernet Adapter into an electrical socket in your spare bedroom

- Connect the computer in your spare bedroom to the Powerline Ethernet Adapter using an Ethernet cable.

The setup above will connect the computer in your spare bedroom to the switch in your study, by effectively using the electrical wiring in your house as an extension to the Ethernet cables connected to the switch and your computers.

If you wanted to add another computer to this network in a different room you could do so by following exactly the same process as you did for the computer in your spare bedroom – you would need a third Powerline Ethernet Adaptor to do this.

So far we have described ways of setting up a local area network, using both cabled and wireless connections. While this is fine for allowing computers in the same building to communicate with each other, how can computers connect to the wide world of the internet? The next section explains this.

Wide Area Networks

A wide area network (WAN) is a network that expands beyond the confines of a single location, allowing computers at different locations to communicate with each other. The best known example of a WAN is the internet, a global network of billions of computing devices. This section explains how computers connect to the internet, and how they can be connected to a local area network at the same time.

How does data travel over the internet?

Given the geographical spread of the internet, connecting several billion devices together using Ethernet cable clearly isn't feasible. Nor is the option of wi-fi, as even the strongest wi-fi radio signals would struggle to cover a distance of more than 100 metres. So how can data from a computer in one location travel thousands of miles to a computer on another side of the world?

The answer is that the data can use multiple forms of transport as it travels across the world. These include coaxial cable (similar to that used to connect TV aerials), copper wire (including ethernet cables), fibre-optic cables and radio waves.

Let's consider the landscape of the internet. First of all, of the billions of computing devices which are connected to it, very few are *directly* connected together. Instead, they are indirectly connected through devices called *routers*. We have already mentioned routers, and the role that they can play in connecting devices together on a local area network. A router takes a chunk of data arriving on one of its incoming links and forwards it to another location via one of its outgoing links.

When describing the way that data travels over the internet a useful analogy is the journey of a package which is posted from one country to another. The package may start its journey by road, being collected from the customer's home and delivered to a local depot. It is then moved from that depot to a depot close to the nearest airport. From there it is taken by road to the airport and transported by air to the overseas airport. When it arrives at the overseas airport it is transported to a depot near the airport by road. It is then collected and transported by road to a distribution centre close to the final delivery address. From there the final delivery is made by road.

At each stage of its journey the address details on the package are used to determine the next stage of the journey. What's important at each stage is that the package is routed in the right direction, using the most efficient mode of transport.

The journey of data over the internet is similar to this in many ways, except that the modes of transport involve cables, wireless/radio connections and routers instead of roads, airlines and depots. Each chunk of data has an address attached to it, so that it can be guided on its journey to the correct destination.

The example below describes how data might travel from a typical home computing environment to another computer on the internet. This example assumes that the computers at each end are connected to the internet using a technology called ADSL (Asynchronous Digital Subscriber Line), a common internet technology which will be described later.

The first stage of its journey may be to travel via wi-fi from a laptop to a wireless router in the house. This router is typically connected to the telephone system via a cable, so the data travels from the router in your house to the local telephone exchange via the cables used by your telephone system (following the same path that telephone calls use to get to the telephone exchange). This part of the journey – from the router in your house to the telephone exchange – is usually one of the slowest. The method that it uses to travel this part will largely determine how fast you perceive your internet connection to be – the section below on broadband technologies explains the options available for this.

From the telephone exchange it travels to a router in a computing centre run by your internet service provider (ISP). This journey is typically conducted via some sort of cabling infrastructure. From there it travels to a router in a computing centre owned by a larger ISP or network provider, which in turn forwards it to a router in a shared computing centre which is used by many internet service providers. These journeys would also usually happen via some sort of cabling infrastructure.

When it reaches the shared computing centre it may be routed to a shared computing centre in a different country. This journey may be undertaken via fibre optic cables running across an ocean for example. When it arrives in the destination country it follows a similar journey to the one that it took in the originating country, but in reverse. So first it gets passed to a router in the computer centre of a large ISP, then forwarded to a router in a smaller ISP's computing centre. The smaller ISP's router sends it to the nearest telephone exchange to the destination, and from there it is sent to a router at the final destination via the local telephone cables. Once it arrives at this router it makes the final leg of its journey to the target computer via an Ethernet cable connecting the computer to the router.

From the above, you can see that the journey of a chunk of data across the internet involves many steps, mainly travelling between routers at different locations. At each step the address of the data is inspected by the router so that it can determine where to send it for the next stage of its journey. The amazing thing is that each end-to-end journey is usually completed in no more than a few seconds, rather than the days or weeks that a package may take to complete the same journey!

Another interesting characteristic of this journey is that, even if several chunks of data are travelling to the same destination, they may not follow exactly the same path. At each stage of the journey the router handling the data may have options for where to send the data next. In the same way that there may be several roads or airlines connecting two locations, there may also be several computer networks linking two locations. A router will take a number of things into account when deciding where to despatch the data next. As well as the final destination, for example, it may know that one or more of the network links is congested with alot of data and may choose to avoid it for that reason. Likewise it could be that a particular route is not working at all, perhaps due to a power failure at a computing centre, so an attempt might be made to send the data via a different computing centre.

Broadband technologies

The most common way to connect a home to the internet is using technology which is generically referred to as *broadband*. This refers to the ability of a network technology to carry a large amount of data at one time. There are many ways of doing this - most involve some form of cable but some are wireless. This section describes the most common technologies in use for domestic broadband.

Before home broadband was invented the only way for home users to connect to the internet was using "dial-up" technology. This largely used the technologies which were already used for telephone and fax communication, and was both inconvenient and very slow. For example, downloading a song from the internet would take somewhere between 10 and 30 minutes. With broadband technology this time was reduced to less than one minute.

ADSL

Broadband services began to become popular from 2001. The initial service used a technology called ADSL (Asynchronous Digital Subscriber Line), and this remains the most common technology used for home internet connections. The technology uses existing telephone cables to transmit data traffic, but using very a different technique to the one used for dial-up internet connections. Effectively ADSL uses your telephone cable as if it were two separate cables – one for data signals and the other for telephone and fax calls. It does this using equipment which converts data into a signal which can be carried over telephone cables. The equipment is also able to separate the data signals from the telephone and fax signals. All of this means that you can make and receive telephone calls while using the internet at the same time.

In the home, a small adapter called a splitter or microfilter is added to your phone socket. This has two sockets – one for your telephone and one for your broadband equipment. Your broadband equipment will consist of an ADSL modem – this converts computer data into signals which can be transmitted over the telephone line. ADSL modems are often combined with a router in the same piece of dual-purpose hardware.

The signals that ADSL uses to carry data use different frequencies to the ones used to carry telephone calls. ADSL also uses a wider range of frequencies for *downloading* data than it does for *uploading* data. For this reason it is faster to download data via an ADSL broadband connection than it is to upload data (this is where the *Asymmetric* part of the ADSL name comes from).

The other important characteristic of ADSL performance is that is highly dependent on the distance that the data has to travel. In effect this means that the closer you live to your local telephone exchange the faster your ADSL connection will be. ADSL speeds can also be hindered by poor quality or long internal home telephone wiring.

In recent years an improved version of ADSL has been developed. This is called ADSL2, and it is capable of faster data transfer speeds. It can also cover a greater distance over the same telephone cables, as well as being more reliable when the quality of the telephone lines is not ideal.

Cable broadband

Cable broadband makes use of the infrastructure of cable television networks. In these networks, a single cable will deliver the service to a residential area. Customers will each have a connection to that cable. Cable broadband tends to be less common than ADSL because many areas do not have access to a cable television network.

Cable Internet users need a *cable modem* to connect to the service. This in turn is connected to the user's home network via a router, or alternatively to the user's computer with an Ethernet cable. As with ADSL, some suppliers provide a dual-purpose unit consisting of a combined cable modem and router.

Cable has the potential to offer faster speeds than ADSL, as the cabling tends to be of a higher quality and more free of the interference and "noise" which can plague telephone lines.

Fibre broadband

One of the weaknesses of ADSL is the quality of the telephone cabling that it depends on. This is usually a simple pair of copper wires which were never designed to carry high-speed data traffic. This issue is addressed by a more recent entrant to the broadband market: fibre broadband.

Fibre broadband uses fibre optic cable to carry data. As well as being lighter, thinner and more hard-wearing than other types of cabling, fibre optics offer much greater speed and clarity. This can be of enormous benefit when transferring multimedia content over the internet (e.g. videos or internet voice calls). Since fibre optic cables use glass as the transfer medium, which does not conduct electricity, they are not prone to the sort of electrical interference caused by lightning for example which can affect Cable and ADSL services. Fibre optical cabling can also carry data at high speed over much longer distances.

Like Cable networks, many areas do not have access to fibre networks. The cost of laying new fibre cabling is also relatively high. For this reason partial fibre solutions have been explored in some areas. This involves using fibre optic cables to connect the telephone exchange to telephone junction cabinets in streets, but leaving the existing copper telephone cables in place to connect the junction cabinets to customers' homes. This solution is referred to as "Fibre to the Cabinet" (FTTC). The "full" solution, where fibre cabling is used for the entire connection between the telephone exchange and the customer's home, is called "Fibre to the Home" (FTTH) or "Fibre to the Premises" (FTTP).

Even if fibre cabling is only used for part of the distance between the exchange and the customer's home, this will significantly improve performance as it leaves a much shorter distance for the data to travel over inferior copper telephone cables.

When LAN and WAN combine

Up to now we've discussed local area networks and wide area networks as separate entities. In reality they are usually inter-linked.

When a computer needs to interact with another computer the other computer may be in the same building or it may be on the other side of the world. For example, a user may want to copy a document to another computer on the company's local area network. Alternatively, the same user may want to look at a web page which is stored on a computer in another country – this would require the use of a wide area network (i.e. the internet). So how can a computer connect to a local area network and wide area network at the same time?

The answer lies in a device called a *gateway*. A gateway is a type of computing device on a network. It has the ability to receive a chunk of data on a local area network and redirect it to a location on a wide area network (e.g. the internet). A gateway can take a number of forms. For example, it could be built into a router. Alternatively, a computer can act as a gateway by running a program which allows it to do so. In a home computing environment the gateway is usually built into the router that is provided by your internet service provider.

When a computer sends a chunk of data to a specified destination the IP address is first inspected to see if it is an "internal" address – i.e. whether it is in the same local area network as the computer sending the data. If so, it sends the data directly to the destination computer using the local network connections as described above. If the IP address is not internal – e.g. if it refers to a computer somewhere on the internet – then the data is sent to the gateway instead. The gateway then sends the data to the wide area network (e.g. the internet).

So how can you tell whether or not an IP address is "internal"? The answer lies in the first part of the address - certain number ranges are reserved for use by local networks. For example if an IP address starts with any of the following numbers then it will be an internal address:

10.0...
192.168...
172.16...

Any IP addresses which are **not** in the above ranges are called *external* IP addresses, or *public* IP addresses.

The concept of external and internal IP addresses is very similar to the concept of telephone numbers and extension numbers. A telephone number is similar to a public IP address – it must be unique across all locations. An extension number is similar to a local IP address – it only needs to be unique within a specific location. So it's quite likely that a computer on a local area network will have exactly the same internal IP address as a computer on another local area network at a different location.

It may be easier to think of an external IP address being assigned to a particular location (e.g. an office or a home address), while an internal IP address identifies an individual computer within that location.

Why should we need to differentiate between internal and external IP addresses? Why can't every device in the world have its own unique IP address? The reason is very similar to the reason why telephone extension numbers exist - the numbering convention originally invented for telephones didn't allow for enough numbers for every telephone in the world. Likewise the original standard for IP addresses didn't allow for enough numbers for every device which wanted to connect to the internet. The latest standard (IP version 6) will solve this problem, but for now we need to deal with the concept of internal and external IP addresses.

So what happens when a computer in one location wants to communicate with a specific computer in a different location? It may know the external IP address of the location where the other computer sits, but for a number of reasons it will not know the internal IP address of that computer. Why not? Well, for one thing the computers and internal IP addresses at the other location may change from time to time, much like people and their telephone extensions. Exactly which computer has which IP address is something which the local network administrators will manage, but they have no reason to share this information with people from other organisations. It may also be true that their computers have dynamic IP addresses, so the same computer may have a different internal IP address from one day to the next.

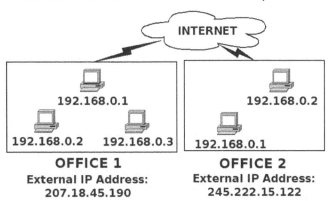

Figure 12: Internet locations and IP addresses

If we go back to the analogy with office telephone systems, this is the equivalent of a person on a telephone extension in a particular organisation wanting to call a person on a telephone extension in a different organisation. To do this they need to dial the public telephone number of the other organisation, then ask the receptionist to connect them to the right person within that organisation. The receptionist looks up the extension number of that person and directs the call to that extension.

Likewise, a computer will need to address its outbound internet data to the public IP address of the other organisation. But who or what will perform the role of the receptionist, directing the data to the correct computer on their internal network? To fully understand this we need to become familiar with *firewalls, ports* and *port forwarding*.

Firewalls, ports and port forwarding

In a typical environment the first device that data encounters when it arrives at a location is a firewall. A firewall is a program which runs on either a computer or a piece of networking hardware. Firewall programs are often built in to routers, or can sometimes run on their own dedicated hardware device. The main function of a firewall is to sit between one part of a network and another, and to stop any unwanted data passing from one side to the other. For example, a firewall is an important way of stopping unwanted data infiltrating a local network from the internet.

It's not unusual to find a number of firewalls on a network. For example, most computers have a firewall program running to restrict the flow of network data either into or out of the computer. This helps to ensure that the computer is not exposed to threats on the network or the internet. Such threats are discussed in more detail in a later chapter.

Another important function of a firewall is to examine incoming data (e.g. from the internet) and direct it to the correct location within an internal network. In order to do this the data needs to contain something which can tell the firewall where it needs to go. One of the most important items in the data that is used for this purpose is the port number. We've already used the word "port" in an earlier chapter to describe a socket or connection – for example the USB ports on a computer, or the Ethernet ports on a switch, hub or router. In the world of computer networking the word "port" has a different meaning however.

In networking parlance, a port is a number which is used to classify or subdivide network data traffic arriving at a computer or location. When a computer sends a chunk of data to another computer a port number is usually included alongside the destination IP address. The port number is a way that the sending computer can influence which computer receives and processes the data at the destination location. While the IP address tells the data which location to go to, the port number is used to direct the data to the correct computer at that location.

Specific port numbers are commonly associated with particular types of data. For example, requests for web pages on the worldwide web usually have a port number of 80. Outbound emails often have a port number of 25. An organisation may have a number of computers on its local network, each performing different roles. One of these computers might be designated as a web server for example– i.e. a computer running a web server program which stores web pages and deals with requests for those web pages from the internet. The firewall will use its knowledge of port numbers, as well as its knowledge of the computers its internal network, to send data to the correct computer. So for example if it comes across incoming data from the internet which has a port number of 80 it will send that data to the computer which it knows to be the web server on its network. This process is called port forwarding.

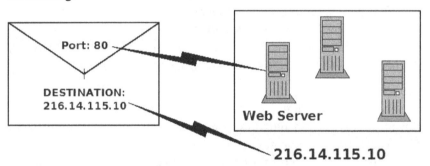

Figure 13:Port forwarding

Port forwarding is a good way of directing data to the correct server on a network. We've referred to the term "server" a few times up to this point. A server is a system that responds to requests that it receives over a network. The senders of these requests are commonly called "clients". If a server is offering a service over the internet - for example a web site - then its public IP address will be widely known so that clients know where to send their requests. Port forwarding then enables requests from clients to be directed to the correct server computer when they reach the public IP address. An interesting dilemma arises when the server wants to send a response to the client however.

As we've seen from the sections above, the internal IP addresses of computers at a location are generally not shared with people at other locations. When data from a computer on a local network is sent over the internet it is sent with a reply address (i.e. an IP address to which responses should be sent) - in much the same way as you might write a reply address at the top of a letter. This reply address is not the internal IP address of the computer sending the data however - it is the external IP address of the location of the computer. So when a server wants to send a response to the client computer that sent a request to it, how can that response find its way back to the specific computer that sent the request, if only the public IP address of its location is known? That public IP address might be shared by other computers at the same location as the client. For example, the client might be one of 100 computers at the same location, all of which share the same public IP address, and all of which might be sending requests to web servers. So how can the response from the server find its way to the client computer that sent the request?

The port forwarding logic described above doesn't help here, because all clients sending requests to web servers will typically use port number 80 in their requests - hence this port number can't be used to trace a request back to a specific computer at the sending location. Instead, a technique called Network Address Translation (NAT) is used.

In much the same way that port forwarding acts as a "receptionist" at the server location - directing data arriving at a public IP address to the relevant server on the network, a Network Address Translation (NAT) service performs this role at the client location. This service is a program which usually runs on a router or firewall device - often sitting alongside the gateway. It keeps track of all requests being sent to the internet by computers on its local network, and ensures that any responses from servers are directed back to the client computer which sent the original request.

Protocols

The types of data that pass over the internet can be many and varied – e.g. emails, pages from websites, TV shows, music, electronic payments or even telephone calls. At a basic level it all looks the same however: it's all binary data - bits and bytes. So how does a computer know what to do with a piece of data when it arrives from the internet, or from the local network? We need a way of categorising and labelling data so that the computer on the receiving end knows what to do with it. One of the most popular ways of doing this is to use protocols.

So what is a protocol? The best way to explain it would be to examine a human protocol that you will already be familiar with. Let's say you are in a restaurant and a waiter arrives at your table. The waiter asks "can I take your order?". You may reply in a couple of different ways. For example, you may say "not yet, we're still deciding", in which case the waiter will go away and return later. Alternatively you may say "yes, please", and then provide the waiter with details of your order. This is an example of messages being exchanged between you and the waiter, and different actions and responses resulting, based on the content of the messages. Both you and the waiter are following a protocol that you are familiar with. In this example there is also another underlying protocol at work: the basic conversational protocol of a person speaking to another person, then waiting for a response.

Computer networks use protocols to define the many different ways that data needs to be handled. For example, there are a number of protocols which are used for handling email (e.g. SMTP, IMAP and POP). Other protocols exist to define how the worldwide web works (e.g. HTTP). There are also major underlying protocols which make things like email and the worldwide web possible (e.g. TCP and IP). These protocols are explored in more detail later.

Port numbers are often closely associated with protocols. So for example the HTTP protocol, used to handle web pages on the worldwide web, is usually associated with port 80. The SMTP protocol, used for sending email, is usually associated with port 25.

TCP/IP

Regardless of the type of data that is being sent, one common theme is that the data will be broken down into very small chunks before it is sent over a network (either a local area network or a wide area network such as the internet). These chunks are called packets. Packets can vary in size, but are often of the order of 1,000 bytes each.

For example, an email might be broken down into dozens of small packets before it is sent over the internet. Each packet will be transmitted individually over the network, and each will have both the sender's IP address and the destination IP address attached to it, so that the routers that it passes through will know which way to send it. This is the equivalent of tearing a letter up into hundreds of small pieces, then posting each piece to the recipient in a separate envelope. Breaking network data into small chunks like this makes it much easier to manage the overall flow of data across networks. If very large chunks of data were sent over a network they could very easily cause congestion - much like very large vehicles on the public road network.

As we have seen above, even though all of the packets in an email for example are going to the same destination, they may not all follow the same path. This means that they may not all arrive at the same time. So how will the computer sitting at the other end deal with the confusion of hundreds of packets all arriving at different times? How will it piece them all together? How will it know when it has received all of the intended data? Well, the sender and receiver (i.e. the sending and receiving computers) will both be familiar with a protocol which describes how data is broken down and transmitted in lots of small packets. This protocol will tell the recipient how to recognise when such a transmission has started, when it has finished, and how it should re-assemble the pieces into their original form. It also covers what to do if a packet gets lost in transit – i.e. if it doesn't turn up at the intended destination. This particular protocol is called TCP (Transmission Control Protocol), and it also covers a number of other areas which help to ensure the smooth running of networks.

Another important protocol which we have already made passing reference to is the Internet Protocol (IP). Amongst other things, this protocol describes how addresses should be attached to individual data packets, what the addresses should look like (see the discussion regarding IP addresses above), and how routers should use these addresses to determine where to send a data packet that it receives.

5 The Worldwide Web

For many people the term "worldwide web" is synonymous with the internet. The two are not the same thing however.

The internet is the collection of billions of computing devices connected together across the world, including the routers and telecommunications links that allow them to communicate with each other. The internet can be used for a multitude of things including email, social networking, voice calls, audio and video conferencing, file sharing and remote working. The worldwide web is subset of the internet which supports a particular type of *usage* of the internet. Specifically, it refers to computers which support a particular type of document. This type of document is commonly referred to as a web page.

While the worldwide web did not come into existence until the early 1990s, it resulted from a number of concepts which were evolved and combined throughout the 1980s. Two of the most important concepts were *hypertext* and *markup languages*.

Hypertext is a technique whereby text displayed on a computer screen can contain links to other text. The user can immediately "jump" to the other text simply by clicking on the link with a mouse, or by selecting the link using a keyboard or touchscreen.

Markup languages are a way of adding information to a document to indicate how the document should look when either printed or displayed on a screen, in terms of its layout, formatting and style. For example a markup language may indicate the font or colour to be used for text, or whether text should be left or right-justified. It can also be used to define other elements of format and page layout such as margins, headers and footers. The most common use of markup languages in the 1980s was by word processing software, which used markup language to describe how documents should appear on a printed page.

The concepts of hypertext and markup languages were merged and evolved into a markup language called hypertext markup language (HTML). This remains the primary language used to define web pages today. HTML allows documents to be defined which contain not only text but also images, videos, and other multimedia. It also allows "hyperlinks" to be defined, which allow the user to jump from one place in the document to another, or to jump to an entirely different document. HTML documents stored on a computer will usually have a file extension of .html or .htm. So for example a web page document may be called mywebpage.html.

So how does an HTML document get converted into a web page that is displayed on a computer screen, with all of the correct text, fonts, images and layout? The answer is a type of computer program called a *web browser*. The purpose of a web browser is to examine an HTML document and translate it into a visual form which it displays to the user. Examples of popular web browser programs are Internet Explorer, Firefox, Chrome and Safari.

Having developed a language for creating web pages, the next step was to make web pages available on the internet – i.e. to allow web pages to be stored on any computer on the internet, and to be accessible from any other computer on the internet. For this to happen, two things were required:

- a naming system which allowed every web page to have a unique name

- a protocol to define how to access web pages over the internet.

Domain Names

We have seen how external IP addresses can identify the locations of computers on the internet. While this works perfectly well, a naming system is a far easier and more logical way to refer to an address on the internet. Fortunately, just such a system exists - it is called the Domain Name System, or DNS.

A domain name is an easy-to-remember way of identifying a location on the internet. It usually consists of at least two parts, separated by a dot. For example:

- google.com

- bbc.co.uk

- harvard.edu

The rightmost part of a domain name is called the top level

domain (TLD). So in the above examples the top level domains are *com, uk* and *edu*. The TLD indicates what type of location the domain refers to - for example:

- com - a commercial organisation

- gov - a US government organization

- org - an organisation

- uk - a location in the United Kingdom

A defined list of top level domains is available for use in domain names. This list is controlled by an organisation based in the USA called ICANN - the Internet Corporation for Assigned Names and Numbers.

To the left of the top level domain can be one or more mid-level domains – google, co, bbc and harvard in the examples above. Typically a mid-level domain name will refer to a particular organisation - Google, the BBC and Harvard University in the examples above. The choice of mid-level domains is much wider, with an almost endless range of names available for use.

Domain names are often prefixed with letters which indicate a particular type of service which is available at a location. For example www.bbc.co.uk refers to the worldwide web service at the BBC in the United Kingdom. Another example might be *mail.yahoo.com*, referring to an email service at the *yahoo.com* domain.

In order for a domain name to be useful there must be some way of associating it with an external IP address. Without this, a message sent to a domain name will have no way of finding its destination. In the same way that we need a telephone directory to look up the telephone number of a named person or organisation, we need a way of looking up an external IP address for a domain name. This lookup service is provided by DNS Servers. A DNS server is a program running on a computer which maintains a list of domain names and their associated external IP addresses. Thousands of computers all over the world run DNS server programs, but a centralised registry of domain names is maintained on a smaller group of designated computers which are called the *root DNS servers*. When a domain is registered it is added to the root servers, and when it expires it is removed from the root servers.

DNS servers operate in a hierarchy, with the root servers sitting at the top of the hierarchy. Beneath them are trusted DNS servers which may contain certain pieces of the overall list. Beneath these will be lower level DNS servers.

When a message is sent to a domain name the first thing that happens is the nearest DNS server is consulted to determine what the external IP address is for that domain name. The nearest DNS server is usually one that is run by your Internet Service Provider. That DNS server will consult a higher-level DNS server to find out what the associated external IP address is. It will then make a copy of this information - this is called "caching". This is extremely important for two reasons - firstly, it will speed up the processing of any future requests for that domain name. Secondly, it will reduce the load on the root servers and other high-level DNS Servers. If a DNS server receives a request for a domain that it has not had before it will need to consult a higher-level server. If that server does not have the required information it may need to consult one of the root servers.

A DNS server does not keep information for a domain forever. Instead, it deletes it after a designated period of time. The next time it receives a request for that domain it will need to consult a higher level DNS server in the hierarchy again. The time that the information is kept can be different for each domain, and is called the "time-to-live" (TTL). This can be anything from a few minutes to several hours. This method of caching, regularly deleting and re-requesting information ensures that lower-level DNS servers can be kept up to date with any new or changed information from higher level DNS servers. However it also means that at any point in time a DNS server may have out-of-date information (for example when an external IP address for a domain has changed). That information will remain out-of-date for a domain until the TTL period expires, and the information is refreshed from a higher-level DNS server which has been told about the change.

HTTP - a protocol for the worldwide web

We have already discussed how *protocols* are used to tell computers how to deal with the billions of items of data that flow around the internet. The worldwide web is no exception. In this case the most important protocol is called Hypertext Transfer Protocol (HTTP).

HTTP works on the principle of a request and a response. First of all, a user sends a request to the computer on which a web page is stored.

They do this by typing the address of the web page into their web browser. The most popular way of entering an address is to use a convention called a Uniform Resource Locator (URL). While a domain name can identify a particular location on the internet, a URL allows you to identify a specific resource at a location - for example a specific web page.

A URL consists of three parts:

- Network protocol - the protocol which will be used to access the resource. The protocol name in a URL is always followed by these three characters: "://"

- Domain name - the full domain name, including both mid-level and top-level domains

- File or resource name - the name of a specific resource at the domain, for example a web page. This might include a folder name if the resource is located in a folder.

An example of a simple URL is:

http://myinternetplace.com/myfolder/mywebpage.html

The URL above contains the address of a web page - this is indicated by the http:// at the start of the address. The web page document is called mywebpage.html, and is stored in a folder called myfolder at the domain called myinternetplace.com. Since web sites normally use the HTTP protocol most web browsers allow the user to omit the http:// prefix – the browser will assume that the URL requires this prefix. Another commonly used protocol on the worldwide web is HTTPS – this is a more secure variation of the HTTP protocol, and is described in detail in the Security chapter.

The web browser sends the full URL to the target computer (having first looked up the external IP address for that domain using a DNS server). The target computer will be running a special type of program called a *web server*. When the target computer receives the request the web server program looks for the web page that is being requested and sends the contents of the page (e.g. an HTML document) back to the user's computer as its *response*. The user's web browser interprets the contents of the HTML document and uses it to display the web page to the user.

So why is it that when we request a web page we usually only enter the domain name, and not the name of a web page? For example if we simply enter *myinternetplace.com* in our web browser we will get a web page returned to us, even if we didn't specify the name of the web page that we wanted at the *myinternetplace.com* address? The answer is that, if you don't specify a particular web page when you send a request to a web server, the web server makes an assumption about the name of the web page that you want to see. The assumption that it makes depends on the type of software running on the web server. For example, many web servers will send a page called *index.html* back to a user if they specified a domain name but no specific web page name in their request. Pages like this are sometimes referred to as *default* pages.

It's interesting to note that, while the DNS makes it much easier to remember the addresses of places on the internet, you can usually use an IP address instead of a domain name and it will work just as well. For example, if you type this address into a web browser:

    173.194.41.69

You will probably get a Google search page returned. This is because DNS lists this IP address as being associated with google.com.

DNS is not just used by the worldwide web. It can be used by any service that uses the internet. For example, email systems make extensive use of DNS to direct their data traffic over the internet.

When web pages are more than web pages

When the worldwide web was first created it was concerned only with the display of published information. It was an alternative way of finding and viewing information which up to that point had only been available in printed form – e.g. in academic journals, newspapers, magazines and books.

As the worldwide web became more widely used it began to provide more sophisticated features. This began with the introduction of *forms* in web pages. Forms allowed users to enter information into web pages and to send that information back to the web server. When the information arrived at the web server it was processed and a new page was generated and sent back in response.

This simple model of data being entered into a web browser and sent to a web server for processing is the basis for what are now called *web applications.* A web application is a program running on a web server which takes input from a user via a web browser. Many of us use web applications quite frequently – for example to purchase items from online retailers, or to manage our bank accounts online.

In the above model for web applications all of the processing logic is executed on the web server. The user's web browser is not involved in executing any of this logic – it simply displays the pages returned from the web server. This approach has its limitations. For example, if the data that you enter into a web browser is incorrect it will be sent to the web server, found to be incorrect, and a page will be returned to you explaining why your data is incorrect. This can waste time, as you have to wait for the data to be sent to the web server, the processing to take place, and the page to be returned to your web browser before realising that you have made a mistake. In the days before broadband, when data took much longer to travel over the internet, this was a significant problem.

The solution to this problem was to introduce a way for web browsers to handle small processing tasks. For example, if the data to be entered on a form needs to be in a particular format (e.g. numeric) it would be useful if the web browser could check for this *before* sending the data to the web server, and to tell the user to correct the data if there were any problems. The user could then be sure that the data was correct *before* any data was sent to the web server.

This facility became possible with the introduction of a programming language called JavaScript. JavaScript allowed programming logic to be included in web pages, and for that logic to be executed by the *web browser*, rather than the web server. JavaScript became popular very quickly, as it allowed users to interact with web applications much more quickly.

One of the drawbacks of Javascript is that there can be subtle variations in the way that JavaScript programs are executed, depending on the type of web browser that you are using. This can sometimes lead to unpredictable behaviour and errors when opening web pages which make extensive use of JavaScript.

Since the emergence of Javascript other technologies have been developed which also allow programming logic to be carried out by web browsers. These usually involve upgrading the web browser to add what is known as a *plug-in*. Each plug-in enables programming instructions to be executed which have been written using a particular programming language. Rather confusingly, one such language is called Java (this is not to be confused with Javascript!). Another type of plug-in (specific to Microsoft software) is called ActiveX.

A plug-in is a processing "brain" which you install into your web browser. When you visit certain types of web site they may contain programming instructions which can be executed by the associated plug-in. For example, a web page may contain logic written using the Java language, and this logic can be executed by the Java plug-in installed in your web browser. These plug-ins have become more and more popular in recent years as web applications aim to offer users more advanced features.

While Javascript and plug-ins have done alot to improve the features which can be offered by web sites, there are significant drawbacks relating to *security* – this is discussed later in the chapter dedicated to security.

6 Email

As well as the worldwide web, one of the most popular uses of the internet is for email. Most of us will be familiar with email as a way of exchanging messages with recipients far and wide. You will not be surprised to know that most email traffic finds its way across the world using the same transport mechanisms as described above. Like the worldwide web, email is another way of using the internet to exchange data between computing devices in different places.

In the early days of email it was only possible to exchange messages with people working in the same organisation. For example, colleges and businesses may have had internal email services which operated entirely over their local area networks.

As the internet became more established, and more organisations became connected to it, it became common for organisations to extend the reach of their email service by allowing messages to be exchanged with other organisations on the internet.

Today email is available to anyone who has access to an internet connection. There are a number of different ways of sending and receiving emails, and a number of different protocols which may be used. The most popular protocols are described below.

Before discussing email protocols however we must understand the concept of a **mail server**. This is a computer running a program which manages the sending, receiving and storage of emails. A mail server can be thought of as similar to a post office - a place where mail can be sent or collected. It also performs a similar role to a sorting office – it receives and sorts incoming mail.

There are millions of mail servers currently in operation on the internet. Larger organisations are likely to have their own mail server. Smaller organisations may use shared mail servers which provide email services to a number of different organisations. Some organisations have mail servers which are available for use by the general public - these are usually companies operating within the IT industry. For example Google provides mail servers to the general public as part of its Gmail service. Likewise Microsoft provides mail servers to support its Hotmail service. It is also common for internet service providers to provide a mail server for use by their customers.

Each mail server provides an email service for one or more domains *(we have already covered the concept of *domains* as the naming system for places on the internet). The mail server provides a number of *mailboxes* for each domain, each of which can be assigned to an individual or perhaps a department within a company. A mailbox can be thought of as a folder containing all emails sent to the same recipient. Incoming emails addressed to that recipient are stored in their mailbox.

Each mailbox will have the following associated with it:

- A dedicated *email address*

- A user name (sometimes called an account name)

- A password.

Anyone wanting to access a mailbox will need to provide both the user name and the password to do so.

A typical email address will look like this:

person.name@someplace.com

There are two parts to this address:

- The part after the "@" is the domain name

- The part before the "@" refers to the recipient within the domain. This is usually a user name.

So how can users make use of mail servers to send and receive email? There are two main ways of doing this:

- Using a web application (running on the mail server)

- Using a dedicated email program – e.g. Microsoft Outlook.

If you use a web application to access email then all of your interaction with the mail server is done using a web browser (in a similar way to browsing a web site). Email web applications usually provide you with a simple way of sending and receiving emails, as well as browsing and filing emails. This way of using email will be familiar to anyone who has used Gmail or Hotmail.

A dedicated email program means a program installed on your computer which you run if you want to read, send or receive emails. The most popular dedicated email program on the market is Microsoft Outlook, although other programs are also available (Thunderbird, for example). If you use a dedicated mail program then there are several different ways that the program can interact with mail servers, and several different protocols which may be used.

Sending emails: the SMTP protocol

The most common protocol used for sending email messages is called Simple Mail Transfer Protocol (SMTP). It will be used by a dedicated email program which wants to send an email.

When you send an email using your email program it sends a message to the mail server for your domain. This message includes the email addresses of both the sender and the recipient, as well as the contents of the email.

The mail server examines the message, takes the "to" address (e.g. john.smith@somecompany.com) and breaks it into the two parts described above: the recipient name (john.smith) and the domain name (somecompany.com). If the "to" and "from" addresses both include the same domain name (i.e. the sender's address was also someone @somecompany.com), the mail server will simply store the message in the mailbox that it has for the user name of john.smith.

If the recipient's email address is on a different domain then the mail server uses the DNS system described above to translate the domain name into an external IP address, then sends the email to that IP address over the internet. At this stage the first part of the email address (the recipient name) is not important – the email first has to find its way to the relevant domain.

When the email arrives at the destination domain it will be directed to the mail server for that domain. This mail server will act as the sorting office for the email, using the recipient name in the email address to store it in the appropriate mailbox.

Receiving emails: POP vs IMAP

We have seen how emails are sent from dedicated email programs, and find their way into mailboxes at their destination. We can now examine how an email program can retrieve email from a mailbox.

When your email program retrieves an email from the mail server it can either download the email from the mail server to your computer, and (usually) delete it from the mail server, or just allow you to read the email contents from the mail server without saving it on your computer – much like viewing a web page on a web server.

In the first case, where you download an email to your computer, your email program uses a protocol called Post Office Protocol (POP) when communicating with the mail server. This is how the POP protocol works for retrieving emails:

- At regular intervals your email program starts a communication with your domain's mail server, asking if any new emails have arrived for you. At the start of this communication the user name and password for your mailbox is passed to the mail server

- The mail server checks how many emails have arrived for you, if any.

- If any messages are waiting for you it retrieves each one in turn, and sends it back to your email program. It also marks the email for deletion from the mail server's storage, unless your email program has instructed it not to delete emails after they have been retrieved.

- Your email program stores all of your new emails in a folder on your computer

- When all new emails have been sent back to your email program the mail server deletes any of the messages from its storage which have been marked for deletion.

The basic premise of the POP protocol is that, like a post office, the mail server acts as a temporary holding area for your emails until you have downloaded them. One of the benefits of this approach is that you don't need to be continuously connected to the internet while you are reading your emails. For example, if you are going on a journey where you will not have access to the internet you can retrieve your new email messages before you leave (while you are connected to the internet) then read them at any time later. You will not need to be connected to the internet to read them because your email program has stored them in a folder on your computer.

Likewise if you send emails while you are travelling the email program keeps your outbound emails in a folder on your computer, and sends them to your mail server (using SMTP) the next time you are connected to the internet. When the mail server receives them it will send them to their final destination.

When using the POP protocol it is usually a good idea to remove emails from the mail server after you have retrieved them. Most mail servers impose a limit on the amount of email that they will store for you, so if you don't delete email from the server after retrieving it you will eventually exceed this limit. Email programs usually provide options for whether email should be deleted from the mail server after they have been retrieved, including an option to delete emails from the mail server after a certain period of time (e.g. 2 weeks).

One major constraint of using POP is that if you access your email from more than one computer things can get complicated very quickly. Each time that you retrieve your new messages from the mail server they will be downloaded to whichever computer you are using at the time. They will also usually be deleted from the mail server. When you switch to using another computer you will not be able to see the emails that you downloaded onto the first computer that you were using.

To some extent you could work around this problem by choosing to leave your emails on the mail server for a period of time (say 2 weeks), and ensuring that you retrieve them on *all* of your computers during this time. This *should* ensure that all of your computers have a copy of your emails stored on them, but you may not find this a very convenient way of managing your emails.

The final thing to remember when using the POP protocol is that you are responsible for keeping backup copies of the emails that you have retrieved from the mail server. Because permanent copies of your email will not normally be stored on the mail server this means that the emails stored on your computer will be the only copies in existence. Instructions for keeping copies of the emails on your computer will vary depending on which email program you use. For example, Microsoft Outlook stores emails in files with an extension of .PST, so you will need to take backup copies of these .PST files to ensure that you don't permanently lose them.

The other way of retrieving emails is to leave all of your emails on your domain's mail server, and to view them without downloading them to your computer. The most common way of doing this is to use the

IMAP protocol.

In many respects IMAP is similar to using a web application to manage your email. In both cases your emails are stored on the mail server, rather than your computer. The main difference is that you use a dedicated email program, rather than a web browser, to access them.

A useful feature of IMAP is that it allows you to create folders on the mail server, to help you to organise your email. IMAP also allows access to shared mailboxes, which can be an easy way for several people to share information. Each person can connect to the same mailbox on the same mail server, and they will all be able to see everyone else's activities in that mailbox – e.g. incoming and outgoing messages, folders which have been created, etc.

IMAP is primarily intended for those who have continuous access to the internet - i.e. those who are working from a fixed location with internet access, rather than those who move from place to place and may not have internet access at all times. Since your emails are not stored on your computer they will not be accessible unless you are connected to the internet. However many email programs allow you to work around this constraint by offering an option to allow "offline access" to IMAP email. When this option is selected your email program keeps a copy of your emails on your computer, so that you can continue to read them even when you are disconnected from the internet.

IMAP clearly has a number of advantages over POP, particularly if you access your email from more than one computer. The fact that the emails are primarily stored on the mail server, rather than one of your own computers, means that you will get the same view of them regardless of which computer you use to access your email. The main disadvantage is that, because all of your email is retained on the mail server, you can quickly reach the server's email storage limit. This means that you will need to delete older emails on the mail server if you want to stay within your limits. If you want to keep a permanent copy of your older emails most email programs provide a way of copying them to "offline folders" – i.e. folders stored locally on your computer.

In general, the advantages of IMAP make it preferable to POP as a way of managing your email.

Email the Microsoft way

Aside from IMAP and POP there is another option for managing email – this is a proprietary method called Messaging Application Programming Interface (MAPI). This method is exclusive to Microsoft's email server software, which is called Exchange. It is quite common to see Exchange and MAPI used in corporate environments, where Microsoft Exchange is the most popular mail server program.

Microsoft Exchange does not use POP or IMAP for message retrieval. Like IMAP, all emails are stored on the Exchange mail server, and they can be accessed using a compatible email program (such as Microsoft Outlook). Users also have the option of keeping a copy of their emails on their computer however – this is called "cached mode".

Email programs do not use SMTP to send messages to Exchange mail servers – they use an Exchange-specific protocol for this. However Exchange mail servers do use SMTP for sending messages *from one mail server to another.*

Exchange has the added advantage of managing calendar and contact information as well as emails – these are stored and made accessible to compatible email programs such as Outlook.

Anatomy of an email

To many people an email message is quite simple – it's usually a bunch of words, accompanied by a subject line. There's actually more to an email than you might think however. Below we will look at the constituent parts of an email, and why they are important.

First of all, an email has a *header*. This is something which you would not normally see, but which contains information about how the email was transported from the sender to the recipient. This includes the reply address specified by the sender, as well as the email address of the recipients. It also includes details of when each internet site received and forwarded the email to the next location on the internet - this header information is changed each time it passes through an intermediary site. Using the header information you can see what path was taken by the email as it travelled across the internet, and how long it took each intermediary site to process it.

The next component of the email is the message proper, and contains the content which is usually of interest to the user. This will contain a few header fields, such as the email addresses of the sender and recipient, the date that the email was sent, and the subject line. The body of the email will follow this, and will first include information about whether the email is *multi-part*.

A multi-part email is one which contains a mixture of different types of content. For example, in recent years it has become popular to send emails which are written using HTML – the same language that is used to create web pages. This allows emails to contain sophisticated content and formatting, including different colours, fonts and images. While it is fine to use HTML to create an email, the problem is that not all email programs are able to make sense of emails if they are written in HTML – they may only be capable of reading messages which are written in plain text. For this reason it is common for two versions of the email content to be sent in the same email message – one in HTML format and the other in plain text format. This can be done using a multi-part email – the first part could be the plain text version and the second part could be the HTML version.

Another reason for a multi-part email would be if a file was attached to it such as a digital photo or video file, or a word processing document - each attached file would be a separate part of the email.

A standard called MIME (Multipurpose Internet Mail Extensions) is used in the body of an email to indicate whether an email has multiple parts and if so, what type of content is included in each part of the email. This enables the program reading the email to identify the various parts, and to process them in the correct way when it presents them to the reader of the email.

7 Security

Security - it's quite a small word, but an enormous topic. This entire publication could easily have been devoted to security, and particularly its implications for internet users.

At a basic level, the purpose of security in IT is to prevent the wrong people getting access to information. In the days when most "private" information was recorded in paper form, a strong filing cabinet with a key was the most popular way of implementing security. These days a wealth of private information is stored on computers, and most computers are connected to the internet in some way. This has created lots of new ways that private information can fall into the wrong hands, and lots of new measures to prevent it.

It's important to note that there are limits to the help that technology can provide with security. The weakest links in any security measures are often not related to technology. For example, you may have created the longest, most complex password imaginable for your computer, but if you write it on a post-it note and stick it on your computer's screen then you've wasted your time. Likewise if you walk away from your computer after using it for a while, and the screen is visible to anyone who walks past, then any passer-by may have access to your personal documents.

The purpose of this chapter is to provide an overview of the main issues of relevance to home computing and internet users, and to describe some of the associated technologies. It describes some of the more common types of threats, and some of the most common techniques for dealing with those threats.

Encryption

Before we go any further we need to briefly explain the principle of *encryption*, as it plays a central role in many security measures. The basic idea of encryption is that you can take a piece of information and scramble it up so that it is no longer recognisable. If you want to make sense of it again you need to unscramble it – this is called decryption.

The process of scrambling and unscrambling can take many different forms, but there are often two important ingredients:

- A **key** – this is a piece of random data

- An **algorithm** – a piece of logic which uses the key to scramble the information to be encrypted.

This is best explained by way of a very simple example. Let's say that we want to encrypt the following word: **UNIVERSE**

We will encrypt it using the following ingredients:

- A key which contains the following characters: BA8DC47F2EHGJILK5N0MP9ORP6TSVUX3W1ZY

- An algorithm which consists of this logic:

    o Reverse the order of the characters in the word to be encrypted – this will make **ESREVINU**

    o Replace each character in this word with the character to the *left* of the same character in the key. So for example the letter **U** would be replaced by **V**.

Applying this logic will result in **2TO2SJ5V.** So the encrypted form of the word UNIVERSE becomes 2TO2SJ5V.

You can see that even this very simple process can make the original word completely unrecognisable. In this case you can decrypt this encrypted text to discover the original word by simply reversing the logic of the algorithm, provided you know the key. This type of algorithm is called a *symmetric* algorithm – i.e. the logic used to do the encryption can be reversed to perform the decryption.

The methods of encryption used in the real world are infinitely more complex than the one described in the example above. Some algorithms work in such a way that the key that you use to encrypt the data is different to the one that you need to decrypt it – this is called *asymmetric encryption*. These types of algorithm often work in such a way that only one of the keys needs to be kept secret – this is called the *private* key. The other key is called the *public* key. This technique is called **public key encryption.** Even if someone knows what the public key is, they will not be able to use it to decrypt the data – this can only be done using the private key.

The concept of encryption underpins a lot of the techniques which are used to keep computer systems and networks secure – these are discussed later in this chapter.

The dangers of networks

The most common form of IT security is access control – i.e. controlling who has access to a particular computer, website, email account, or other resource. The most common way of implementing access control is with a user name and password.

In a simple environment, with a single computer which is not connected to the internet, or any other type of network, the most important thing is that you use passwords to protect access to your computer and data, keep your passwords safe, and never reveal them to anyone. When you type in a user name and password they are communicated only between you and your computer.

When your computer is connected to a network this situation changes dramatically. Depending on which user name you are using, and what you are using it to access, when you enter your user name and password they could both be transmitted over either a local network or over the internet. For example, if you are entering your user name and password for your internet banking service then they will be transmitted to your bank's computers over the internet so that the bank can check that they are correct. This introduces a whole new dimension from a security point of view.

To use an analogy – let's say that you are having a private conversation with a friend. If you and the friend are together in a room, with nobody else around, you could probably ensure the privacy of your conversation. If however you are talking on the telephone then there is a risk that somebody else might be "listening in". The same applies to computer networks: as soon as your computer is "talking" with another computer over a network (e.g. the internet) there is a chance that someone else might be "listening in".

We have already seen how data packets can travel from a computer at home to another computer, either in the same building or on the other side of the world. It can travel over cables and radio waves, sometimes over very long distances. When you login to your internet banking service for example the data packets containing your user name and password can travel long distances before they reach their destination at the bank's computer. While they are travelling they are at risk of being inspected at various stages of their journey by unwanted intruders.

So how can these intruders inspect your data? Surely the data is safe when it is speeding through an ethernet cable or telephone cable? Surely it's safe when it is travelling from your computer to your wireless router only a few feet away? Sadly this isn't true.

Let's consider the safety of data while it is travelling over cables. At various stages on its journey the data will pass through the staging posts that we discussed in an earlier chapter – for example it may pass through a router in a computer centre. While it travels through that environment there will be opportunities for it to be inspected by someone working at the data centre, using software programs which can inspect data packets passing through the equipment on their network. If they inspect your data packets they will not only be able to see your user name and password, but also the internet address of the place that they are being sent – i.e. your bank. Armed with this information, they could easily access the banking service themselves and use your details to login. These are commonly known as "man in the middle" attacks.

Even outside of data centres, data travelling via cables is susceptible to unwanted interception. For many years a technique called "wire tapping" was used to secretly monitor telephone calls by attaching electronic "probes" to telephone cables, connected to listening equipment. The same techniques exist today to intercept internet data traffic, and there is increasing evidence of its widespread use by government security agencies for example.

Now let's consider the safety of data while it's travelling over radio waves from your computer to your wireless router. While the data may only have a short distance to travel to the router, it actually travels further than you think. The nature of radio signals is that they are "broadcast" to a wide area. In the case of wi-fi this "wide area" is probably no more than 50 metres in radius, but depending on where your computer is located this may well extend beyond the boundaries of your home for example. Any radio receiver within that area could receive the signal (in this case your data). So while the intended destination of your radio-bound data may be your wireless router only a few feet away, in reality any suitably-equipped radio receiver within a

50 metre radius of your computer could pick up your data. If that radio receiver was connected to a computer running the right software program then your data could be inspected by the user of that computer.

While the idea of someone intercepting your wireless data traffic sounds more like something that the intelligence services might do, the technology required to do this is not only widely available but also surprisingly cheap.

Making networks safer

So now that we've established how dangerous it is to send data over a network, why on earth does anyone do it? The answer is that it can be made **a lot** safer using encryption. We've seen how a piece of data can be made completely unrecognisable if it is *encrypted*. Well, if we encrypt a piece of data *before* we send it over a network then, even if it is intercepted using one of the methods described above, it will be of no use to the intruder as they will not be able to make any sense of it. Only if the intruder knows the key that was used to encrypt the data (as well as the algorithm used) will they be able to decrypt it.

Of course this would only be effective if the recipient of the data (e.g. your bank) knew the encryption key. Otherwise they would also be unable to decrypt the data. Fortunately, there is an ingenious way that two parties communicating over the internet can agree on an encryption key, and in a way that the key can't be worked out by a "man in the middle" who is eaves-dropping on the internet. This technique is called Diffie-Hellman, and is based on mathematics originally devised by the GCHQ British intelligence agency in 1976.

Diffie-Hellman works on the principle that each party starts with a common number, which they both know. Each party then generates their own random number, which is not known by the other party. Using basic mathematics, each party raises the common number to the power of its own random number, and sends the result to the other party. The other party takes this result and raises it to the power of its own random number. Magically, the end result obtained by both parties will be exactly the same, and this can be used as a key for encrypting data that is sent between them. To illustrate this using a simple example.

The example below is a simplification of Diffie-Hellman logic, which involves a few more calculations. The mathematics involved in Diffie-Hellman means that any "man in the middle" who sees the numbers being passed between the two parties has no way of guessing the end result that the two parties have both independently calculated, even if they know the common number which both parties started with. This makes it an excellent way of creating a shared secret key.

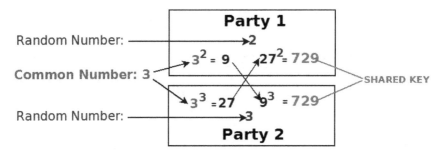

Figure 14:Diffie-Hellman example

So how does this sort of logic get applied in the real world, to encrypt and protect data which is sent over a network? The answer is that it is used in many different ways, some more simple than others, but there is one method which is by far the most popular way of encrypting data which is sent over the internet. This is called Secure Sockets Layer (SSL), also known as Transport Layer Security (TLS).

SSL is another example of a protocol. In this case the protocol defines how data can be encrypted and passed between two places over a network. The SSL protocol is usually implemented by your web browser program, which in turn is communicating with a web server somewhere else on the network, or on the internet.

The following concepts are central to the way that SSL works:

- An SSL certificate – this confirms the identity of the organisation that you are exchanging data with

- Public and private keys – these are used to encrypt and decrypt data passed between you and the organisation.

An SSL certificate is a computer file stored on a web server which vouches for the identity of the organisation that runs the web server. SSL certificates are issued by trusted organisations called Certificate

Authorities. Certificate Authorities are responsible for verifying the identity of organisations running web servers. An SSL certificate links the organisation with the address of its website (e.g. the domain name).

When an organisation obtains an SSL certificate it generates both a public and a private key at the same time, and the private key is also associated with the SSL certificate. These keys are also small computer files, containing scrambled data which makes little sense without the associated encryption logic.

When you want to use the SSL protocol to connect to a web server you indicate this in the URL that you enter into your web browser: instead of starting with http://, you start it with https:// - the extra "s" indicates that you want a secure HTTP connection.

When you enter an *https* URL into your web browser the process below is initiated by your web browser:

- The browser sends your HTTPS request to the web server

- The web server sends a response containing its SSL certificate and its public key

- The web browser receives the SSL certificate and checks whether it is legitimate - i.e. whether or not it can "trust" the web server:

    o it checks that the certificate was issued by an organisation that it knows and trusts (web browsers maintain an internal list of such organisations)

    o it checks that the certificate is still valid and has not expired

    o it checks that the certificate relates to the web site/domain that it is contacting

- The browser generates a random key of its own, and uses the public key it received from the web server to encrypt it. It then uses its own key to encrypt the URL and any other data that it wants to send to the web server. Finally it sends the key, the encrypted URL and all of the encrypted data to the web server

- The web server decrypts the key it has been sent (i.e. the one generated by the browser) using its private key, and uses this key to decrypt the URL and other data

- The web server sends back the requested data (e.g. a web page) encrypted with the key it has been sent

- The browser decrypts the data using the key that it sent to the web server, and displays the information.

Once the steps above have been completed your computer can continue to exchange encrypted data with the web server using the SSL protocol until you close your browser.

SSL is one of a number of ways of using encryption to protect data from prying eyes as it travels over networks. It is most commonly used when using web applications, and needs to be explicitly initiated by prefixing URLs with *https://*.

When SSL is not being used data sent over the internet will travel "in the clear" – i.e. without being encrypted. It's important to note that this also applies to emails, so it is generally not advisable to include sensitive information in emails. If you need to ensure the privacy of data that you send via email then you must find a way of encrypting the content of the email before you send it, and ensuring that the recipient has the necessary algorithm and key to decrypt it. There are a number of ways of doing this, each requiring the use of specialist software. Such software may either be used to encrypt *attachments* to emails (i.e. files that you have attached to the email) or to encrypt the entire email – including both the body text of the email as well as all attachments.

Wireless security

We have discussed how data travelling wirelessly can be vulnerable to unwanted interception and inspection. For this reason it has been become common for wireless devices to include security features to allow data to be encrypted when it is travelling to or from the device.

The option to use wireless security is chosen when you first install and configure a wireless router or wireless access point. If you select this option, you need to enter a key which will used by the encryption algorithms. Any device wanting to connect to it (e.g. a laptop) will be required to supply this key the very first time it connects. Subsequent connections will usually "remember" the key that was supplied, so that you don't need to enter it more than once.

This key may be used in a number of different ways, depending on what encryption protocol is used by your wireless device. There are three main encryption protocols in use today, each of which is described below:

Wireless Encryption Protocol (WEP)

This was the first encryption protocol to become popular on wireless devices. It uses the key that you supply, in conjunction with a complicated algorithm, to generate a different encryption key for *every single packet of data* that travels to or from the wireless device. Each data packet travelling to or from the wireless device is encrypted by the sending device, and decrypted by the receiving device, using the data packet's unique key.

However due to some technical flaws in the design of the WEP protocol it is possible to work out what the encryption key is if you capture and examine a very large number of data packets being sent over the wireless network. In fact it has been demonstrated that this can be done in less than a minute, by examining less than 100,000 data packets.

Wi-Fi Protected Access (WPA)

Weaknesses in WEP led to the emergence of a new protocol called Wi-Fi Protected Access (WPA). WPA uses the same principle of generating a different encryption key for every single data packet, based on the original key that the user supplies, but WPA uses much more complex logic to generate these keys. This makes it virtually impossible to work out the encryption keys, even if an unfeasibly large number of data packets are captured and inspected.

There are different variants of WPA. The most common variant for home and small office networks is called WPA-PSK (Pre-Shared Key) – also known as WPA-Personal. To encrypt a network with WPA2-PSK you provide your wireless router not with an encryption key, but rather with a plain-English passphrase - this is the "pre-shared key". This can be up to 63 characters long. This passphrase is used by a complex algorithm to generate a unique encryption key for each device that connects to it. These encryption keys also constantly change! When you want to connect to the wireless router for the first time from a computer you will need to enter the same passphrase that you entered on the router.

There is a more secure variant of WPA, known as WPA-Enterprise, which is used in larger corporate environments. This does not use a pre-shared key, but instead uses a program running on a computer server to generate a unique key for each computer which wants to connect to the wireless device.

Since its introduction WPA has been improved to use more secure encryption algorithms. The latest version is WPA2. Like WPA, this has both Personal and Enterprise versions, with the personal version including the use of pre-shared keys.

Wireless – other security considerations

When setting up a wireless network in the home it is often tempting to get through the process as quickly as possible, in order to get up and running. This is usually not the best approach however, as it can introduce a number of risks. When you first install a wireless router or wireless access point there are a number of things that you really should do to improve the security of your wireless network.

Firstly, your wireless device will require a user name and password if you want to change any of its configuration settings. To configure these devices, the manufacturers usually have a web application built into the device. This means that you can connect to the device by typing its IP address into a web browser and get access to the configuration options. You must first enter the user name and password however. The user names and passwords for most manufacturers' wireless devices are usually the same, and are easily discovered by searching the internet. For this reason the first configuration setting that you should change should be the password for accessing your wireless router. If you don't do this then anyone within range of your wireless router could connect to it using a web browser, enter the commonly known user name and password, and change its configuration settings – for example to change the encryption that you have entered.

The next configuration setting worth changing is called the SSID (service set identifier). This is a short name which is used to identify your wireless network. Manufacturers usually supply their products with the same SSID, often one which identifies the manufacturer. For example, wireless routers made by Linksys normally have an SSID of "linksys".

The SSID is usually broadcast so that it is visible to anyone nearby who is scanning for a wireless network. By not changing your SSID you are signalling that you have not taken much care in setting up your wireless network, and anyone finding this may be more likely to try to "break in" as a result. For an added level of security you could also choose to **not** broadcast the SSID.

Another option worth considering is called MAC Address Filtering. Every piece of networking equipment has a unique identifier called the physical address or MAC address. Wireless routers and access points keep track of the MAC addresses of all devices that connect to them, and many of them offer an option to restrict access to a list of devices that you specify – in this instance you would identify all such devices using their MAC address. While this is a good thing to do, it is worth knowing that network devices can quite easily fake their own MAC addresses, to impersonate other devices. Hence this will not deter the more sophisticated hacker.

Finally, the positioning of your wireless router or access point can be used to improve security. The signals from these devices usually reach beyond the exterior of a home, and the further it reaches the easier it is for people outside your home to gain access to it. Try to position your wireless router or access point as centrally as possible in your home, to minimise the "leakage" of signal outside your property.

Danger on the internet

Most people are familiar with the term *virus* to describe a malicious program that can do damage to a computer. There can be a tendency to label any internet-borne threat simply as a virus however, when in fact there are many types of threat which can infiltrate your computer in different ways. This section will describe some of the more common types of threat.

Internet threats can arrive at your computer in a number of different ways. For example some can be carried via email. Some can be activated by visiting an untrusted website, or perhaps a trusted website which has been compromised. Others can copy themselves to your computer without your knowledge or intervention.

Viruses

A computer **virus** is a malicious program (also known as *malware)* which travels from computer to computer by attaching itself to a file or program. The infected file could infiltrate your computer in a number of ways. It could be attached to an email, or it could be something that you download from a website. It could also simply be copied from another source – for example a CD or memory stick. The effects of viruses can vary in seriousness. Some may be designed purely to irritate the victim, whereas others may cause damage to your programs, files or even your hardware. Some viruses overwrite "good" programs with copies of themselves, so that the user believes that they are executing a trusted program when in fact they are executing the virus program. A virus might also seek to allow malicious users to control your computer remotely, or to use the internet to send information from your computer to an untrusted recipient.

An important characteristic of a virus is that, even if it has found its way onto your computer, it usually cannot damage your computer unless you run or open the malicious file or program that it is attached to. Also, a virus cannot usually be spread without the help of a human – for example forwarding the offending files as attachments to emails, or copying them to another computer via a network or using a removable storage device.

Worms

A **worm** is similar to a virus but unlike a virus, it has the capability to spread from one computer to another without any human action. A worm takes advantage of weaknesses in the built-in features of operating systems which allow data to travel from one computer to another.

While viruses need to attach themselves to a "host" file or program, worms can exist and spread independently. This characteristic gives worms the power to spread much more quickly than viruses, and in doing so makes them capable of causing serious and widespread damage before they are noticed. For example, a worm might propagate by sending a copy of itself to everyone listed in your email address book, and then do the same again for each of the recipients.

The rapid propagation of worms can affect the operation of systems and networks, as they can consume network capacity as well as system processing capacity as they travel and replicate.

Trojan Horses

A **Trojan Horse** is another type of malware. It is named after the famous wooden horse which the Greeks used to infiltrate Troy. This is because it is designed to look like a trustworthy piece of software from a legitimate source. Recipients of a Trojan Horse are tricked into opening it for this reason. When opened it is able to do its damage, which can range in severity but which can include deleting files, or activating or spreading other malware such as viruses. Trojan Horses may also be used to give control of your system to malicious users.

In contrast to viruses and worms Trojan Horses do not spread by infecting other files, nor do they replicate themselves. Trojans require user actions in order to spread – for example opening an email attachment or running a program downloaded from the internet.

Bots

A **bot** is a specific type of program which is able to be controlled remotely by another computer on the internet. The word derives from the word "robot". Bots are programs that can be designed to perform any number of activities, including activities which are normally carried out by humans – e.g. interacting with websites or internet chat services. Bots can be used for legitimate purposes as well as malicious ones.

A malicious bot, like a worm, can replicate itself. As each copy of the bot infects a new computer it connects back to a central computer which acts as a command and control centre for the growing network of bots (known as a *botnet*). When a large botnet has been established it can be used by the controlling computer to initiate broad-based attacks on target computers or networks. For example, it could be used to flood a target computer on the internet with data packets, and hence consume all of that computer's processing capacity to prevent it from carrying out its normal workload. This type of attack is called a *denial of service* (DoS) attack.

Bots can also be used to gather information, for example capturing the keystrokes entered by users, gathering passwords, spying on data packets sent over the network or capturing information from personal documents. The fact that they communicate with a central computer means that they can change their behaviour in response to commands from that central computer. This can make them very versatile and adaptable.

Bots can be good at keeping a very low profile on infected computers, so that users of that computer would not notice them running. For this reason it is not uncommon for bots to remain undetected on computers for several years.

Phishing emails

Phishing emails are a very common threat. These are unsolicited emails which lure the user to a malicious website (often disguised as a trusted website). These emails usually contain clickable links which take the victim directly to the malicious website, which in turn may collect information or deliver some form of malware to the user's computer.

Sometimes even legitimate websites can be compromised by cybercriminals, causing them to transmit malware to visitors. These sites may be compromised by exploiting weaknesses in the underlying web server or web application programs to inject malicious content.

When sending an email it is very easy to "spoof" the sender's address – i.e. to make it appear that the email has been sent by someone else. This technique is often used in conjunction with phishing emails to give the recipient the impression that the email has been sent from a trusted source.

For example, an email may appear to have come from your bank, asking you to click on a link to change your login details. When you click on the link you are taken to a website which looks identical to your bank's website, but which is actually a malicious site. Clickable links in emails can also be disguised to look like links to legitimate websites. For example, you may click on a link which says www.mybank.com, but if you click on it you may be taken to www.somewherebad.com instead. The standard advice for avoiding this sort of threat is never to click on a link in an email.

Adware

Some forms of malware are designed mainly to show advertisements to users. Programs known as Adware will display unwanted advertising, often in the form of pop-up windows on your computer. Adware usually attaches itself to other programs – for example web browsers. More sophisticated Adware programs are capable of tracking your web browsing activity on the internet, and showing advertisements which are tailored to your interests. As well as causing irritation, Adware can significantly slow down the performance of your web browser.

Spyware

Spyware is a type of malware which is designed to spy on the victim's computer. It monitors various types of activity on your computer, usually so that it can send information back to another computer on the internet. This information is then often used to target the victim, either through advertisements or perhaps something more malicious such as phishing emails.

Scareware

The purpose of Scareware is to cause alarm to a computer user in order to persuade them to purchase a product or visit a malicious website. For example, scareware will typically inform the victim that their computer is either seriously damaged or infected with a virus, and encourage them to click on a link to fix the problem. The purpose is usually to defraud the user into purchasing a bogus anti-malware product.

Keyloggers

A keylogger is a particularly powerful threat as it monitors every keystroke that you make on your keyboard. Using this technique for example it is able to steal user names and passwords that you may type. Keyloggers are often features of Trojan Horse malware.

Are cookies bad for you?

Cookies are files on your computer that enable web sites to remember details about you – e.g. who you are, or what you were doing when you last visited the web site. While this may not sound like a very good idea, cookies can actually play an important role in making web sites more usable.

When you visit a website it may send back a small amount of information to your web browser in a cookie. Each time that you visit that site again the contents of the cookie(s) will be sent back to the site. This can tell it what you were doing the last time you visited, for example to allow you to "pick up where you left off". If you have registered an id with that web site it can also allow the web site to recognise you without you needing to re-enter your id.

Cookies cannot carry viruses or damage your computer in any way. However they can be used to build a long-term profile of your web browsing habits. They can also store sensitive information which you may have entered on a web site, such as a credit card number, although this type of issue can be mitigated if the web site in question and the user's browser encrypt cookies before storing or sending them anywhere. This would prevent the contents being read by third parties.

Cookies can be a valuable source of information for advertisers, who may use them to build a profile of the user and hence to target their advertising. Some web sites share the information in cookies with advertising sites for this reason. If you want to avoid this it is possible to change the configuration settings on your web browser to disable cookies, although you should be aware that this might also disable the genuinely useful features of cookies as described above.

How secure is your computer?

In the previous section we described a number of different types of malicious software, or *malware*. A common feature of malware is that it seeks to exploit weaknesses in the software that is already running on your computer.

When operating systems and computer programs are created the main focus is on ensuring that they do the job for which they are intended. In the case of a computer program that means carrying out all of the tasks that the user would want it to perform. In the case of an operating system it means being able to support all of the programs, hardware, storage and networking facilities that are required of the computer. A common failing when creating programs and operating systems is failing to consider how they could be vulnerable to attack by malware.

Exploiting program vulnerabilities

Let's consider a couple of examples of how weaknesses in a program or operating system can be exploited. First let's take the example of a word processing program. An important part of the work that it does is saving the contents of documents that you have written to a storage device such as a hard disk. In the early chapters of this book we have already seen that programs are loaded into RAM so that the instructions in the program can be executed quickly. What if a malware program could overwrite the area of RAM that the word processing program has been loaded into, and change the instructions in the program? So for example, when the contents of a document are written to a hard disk a second copy of the contents is also sent to another computer over the internet? This could effectively "leak" the contents of your documents to a complete stranger on the internet.

It's often also possible to exploit program weaknesses without actually changing their logic. For example, consider a finance program which processes batches of accounting records. It expects to find a numeric value in a certain place in each record, but if the value is not numeric then it may write some text to an error log file whenever this happens. A malicious program – for example a Trojan Horse - could continually send multiple large batches of records to this program, all containing non-numeric values where numeric values are expected. This would cause the program to repeatedly write text to the error log, which would eventually fill up the storage space that the error log is stored on – for example the computer's hard disk.

Web browser vulnerabilities

Web browsers, more than many other types of programs, are typically designed with security in mind. The reason is that they are usually exposed to a range of unknown sites on the internet, and are hence more vulnerable to threats than programs which perform all of their activity within the boundaries of a single computer. Like any other type of program however, web browsers can have flaws which make them vulnerable to attacks.

In a previous chapter we explained how programming instructions from websites could be the executed by a web browser, using either the Javascript language or browser plug-ins. Since these programming instructions are contained in web pages which are sent from other computers on the internet, clearly the potential exists for them to be used as a means of carrying out malicious processing on a user's computer.

Fortunately, web browsers were designed to mitigate this type of threat. They do this by limiting the scope of the things that Javascript and plug-ins are allowed to do. Firstly, web browsers run all Javascript and plug-in programming instructions in an isolated environment called a "sandbox". This means that they are only allowed to perform actions which are related to web activities, and are not able to do things like creating files on your computer for example.

Secondly, the execution of Javascript is subject to what is called the *same origin policy*. This means that Javascript instructions being executed from one web site must be completely isolated from any processing taking place in relation to a different site. So for example if you enter personal details into a website and it is processed by some Javascript from that website, there is no possibility of Javascript from another website that you visit being able to "grab" those details and use them in its own processing.

While the above measures are designed to prevent Javascript and plug-ins from causing harm to users, in reality cyber criminals have found ways to circumvent them. For example, ways have been discovered of "injecting" malicious Javascript instructions into legitimate web sites which then gets downloaded and executed by users' web browsers. Since such instructions have been downloaded from a legitimate site they will be trusted by your web browser and can perform unwanted operations on that site such as requesting the transfer of money. They will also have access to any information that you have entered on that web site – e.g. your user name and password.

The examples above are simplistic scenarios that illustrate how malicious logic could capitalise on loopholes in the logic of a program or operating system to cause damage or inconvenience. The creators of programs and operating systems are constantly finding such loopholes and closing them down by issuing "patches". These patches are newer versions of programs or operating system components which have their logic revised to prevent exploitation by malware. It is important to ensure that any programs or operating systems that you use are always "patched" with the latest updates to ensure that you are getting the maximum protection from malware.

Anti-virus software

Another way of protecting your computer from malware is to install specialist programs which can detect the presence of viruses, Trojan Horses, etc. The most common form of this type of software is called anti-virus software. As the name implies, its purpose is to protect you from viruses, or from malware in general.

Anti-virus software uses a number of different methods to detect malware. For example, viruses are best detected as soon as they arrive on your computer. One way of doing this is by tapping into your email program and inspecting any attachments to incoming emails for signs of malware. Another is to monitor any files downloaded from the worldwide web (using a web browser) for malware. Alternatively, an anti-virus program can step in whenever you copy a file from a removable storage medium - e.g. a DVD or a USB memory stick.

Another way of detecting malware is to check for it every time you open a file, or every time you run a program. If malware is detected in the file or program the anti-virus software will warn you, and prevent the file or program from being opened.

If any malware manages to slip through these detection methods, the final way of detecting it is via periodic scans of all of the storage devices on your computer. This can be quite time-consuming, but is highly recommended to ensure that no malware has infiltrated your computer undetected by other means.

Most modern anti-virus software will offer most if not all of the options above, but it is important to note that they will all have some impact on the performance of your computer, since they will all add some processing workload to your basic computing tasks.

So how does an anti-virus program recognise malware when it sees it? The most common way is to use virus definition files which contain the "signatures" of known malware. These signatures are fragments of files which, if found, indicate the presence of malware in the files. As new malware is discovered every day on the internet it is important that anti-virus software always has up-to-date virus definition files. For this reason your anti-virus program will download new files on a regular basis (often daily). Failure to do this will prevent it from spotting newer viruses which have emerged on the internet.

As well as virus definition files, anti-virus programs use a technique called *heuristics* to detect malware. Heuristics use the behavioural characteristics of known malware to help spot other malware. For example, if an anti-virus program notices that a program is trying to open every program file on your system and change the content of it in some way, it will probably infer that it is some form of malware.

If malware is detected in a file the anti-virus software will stop the file from being opened or executed and move it into "quarantine" to prevent it causing any damage. It may then delete the file automatically or give you the option of opening or running it anyway, if you are sure that you can trust it. So why would you choose to open a file that your anti-virus software has identified as malware? The answer is that the process of identifying malware is not perfect, and can sometimes result in "false positives" – i.e. files which contain a suspicious virus signature but which are actually legitimate and harmless. In some cases anti-virus software can mistakenly identify critical operating system files as viruses, and consequently disable key parts of the operating system. These incidents can often attract a lot of publicity, as they can have a dramatic impact on very large numbers of computers!

An important thing to note about anti-virus software is that there is no single product which is guaranteed to identify all of the possible varieties of malware on your computer. Detection rates vary between products, to the extent that some users actually choose to run more than one anti-virus product on their computers to improve their chances of detection. This can be quite an extreme measure, as the processing overhead introduced by each can have a marked effect on the performance of your computer.

It's a common misconception that firewalls can detect and prevent viruses from reaching computers. This isn't true. It's certainly true that a firewall can prevent all email reaching a particular network or computer – it could do this by rejecting data packets for port 25 (the SMTP email protocol) for example – but a firewall has no way of inspecting individual emails and determining whether they contain viruses.

8 Multimedia

In recent years the use of home computing and the internet has evolved from being primarily focused on business and communications to becoming more heavily used for entertainment purposes. Typical of this is the use of web sites offering "catch-up" TV – playing back recordings of TV shows which you missed when they were broadcast live.

The internet is also being widely used to distribute music, with the ubiquitous *mp3* format becoming pervasive, particularly in portable audio devices.

The age of digital photography is truly upon us as well, with the vast majority of photographs now being captured in digital format and uploaded to home computers for storage and viewing.

The increasing use of home computers for multimedia consumption has brought with it a number of new challenges, not just for computers but for the networks that link them together. This is mainly because multimedia files such as videos, digital photos and music are typically much larger than the text-based documents which were originally prevalent on computers. For example, all of the text in this book would comfortably fit into less than 250 kilobytes, whereas a 3 minute mp3 music file would require more than 10 times that amount.

The larger file sizes are problematic for two reasons: firstly, it means that storage is consumed much more quickly when multimedia content is being stored. Secondly, transferring such content over a network (particularly the internet) can take an extremely long time. Moreover, transferring extremely large files over a network can quickly saturate the capacity of the network and render it un-usable by other users.

Clearly, if a way could be found to reduce the size of multimedia files then the problems of storage space and network transfers might become more manageable. The key to doing this is *compression* – i.e. taking a large chunk of data and making it smaller.

Compression

A number of methods have been devised for compressing large files, each tailored to the type of content in the file. These compression techniques have become popular not just for use with multimedia files, but with almost any type of file that can grow to an unmanageable size.

Compression is a way of representing the contents of a file in a form of shorthand. There are many ways of doing this, and the effectiveness of each depends largely on the type of content in the file. A common technique is to look for repeating patterns in the file content, and to express them in a non-repetitive way.

A simple compression example

To illustrate this, let's look at a very simple example of how we might compress some text. We will use an extract from a famous quote by Winston Churchill:

"We shall fight on the beaches, we shall fight on the landing grounds, we shall fight in the fields and in the streets, we shall fight in the hills"

You'll notice alot of repetition in this sentence. It is 29 words long (115 characters excluding spaces and punctuation), but many of the words and some phrases are repeated. We can list at all of the words and phrases which are used:

1 we shall fight
2 on the
3 beaches
4 landing grounds
5 in the
6 fields
7 and
8 streets
9 hills

So a shorthand way of writing this sentence (again excluding spaces and punctuation) would be:

1 2 3 1 2 4 1 5 6 7 5 8 1 5 9

This comes to 15 characters. If we then add the characters required to store the "dictionary" of words and phrases – including the associated numbers (a total of 78 characters) – this would total 93 characters. This hasn't reduced the size very much (only by 22 characters), but in a much larger piece of text (e.g. a complete book) the space saving could be quite significant.

Compressing a picture

Now let's consider how compression might apply to a different type of file – this time a digital picture. As explained in an earlier chapter, a digital picture is made up of a pattern of tiny coloured dots (pixels). Each pixel will have a number value indicating its colour. Within any picture there is usually a repetition in the pattern of these dots. For example, a picture of the French national flag will have 3 large areas of red, white and blue. If this picture was 600 pixels wide by 400 pixels high it would have a total size of 240,000 pixels, each with a colour value of Red, White or Blue. However if we wanted to express this in compressed form we could reduce this to something like:

(blue x 80,000) + (white x 80,000) + (red x 80,000)

Storing details of the picture in this shorthand form would require significantly less space than storing details of each of the 240,000 pixels individually.

While the example above is very simplistic, most digital photographs contain many blocks of adjacent pixels which are very similar - for example large areas of sky. It is this repetition of patterns which provides to opportunity for the underlying data to be compressed.

Lossy versus Lossless compression

The examples that we've described above are examples of "lossless" compression – i.e. we haven't lost any important information from the original content as it's possible to accurately reconstruct it from its compressed form. There are other types of compression which offer greater size reductions, but at a cost of losing a little of the original content. This is called "lossy" compression.

For an example of how this might work let's consider how a digital picture of an outdoor landscape might be compressed. Such a picture is likely to contain a large area which looks the same – for example the sky, which might be a large area of blue pixels. Despite the fact that it looks the same, however, if you look at the individual pixels you'll probably find that there are several different shades of blue. To make this picture smaller using the kind of techniques explained above you could simplify it so that all of the sky was represented using pixels of the same shade of blue. When you decompress the file again the sky will look a little different – i.e. you won't see the subtle different shades of blue - but the size of the compressed file would be significantly smaller.

Lossy compression techniques generally try to lose only "unnecessary" information – i.e. detail which would not be very noticeable if it was missing. Sometimes the lost information can go un-noticed, but in other cases the difference when the file is uncompressed can be quite marked.

Audio compression

Like the examples above, audio compression usually works on the principle of identifying repeating patterns in the underlying data, and finding a shorthand way of representing that data. In addition to this, lossy audio compression techniques identify areas in the audio spectrum which are inaudible to the human ear, and omit these parts from the compressed file. They may also tend to "merge" sounds which are very similar.

The compression of audio files often stimulates a lot of debate when the subject of lossy compression arises. Many will argue that lossy compression is unacceptable with audio files at it causes too much degradation to the original sound quality. In practice however lossy compression techniques such as mp3 have become very widely accepted by the general public as they have enabled music collections to be stored on increasingly smaller playback devices such as mobile phones.

Video compression

Video compression is becoming one of the most active areas of research for compression, partly because of the growing popularity of video content on the internet, but mainly because video files are the largest type of multimedia files.

As explained in an earlier chapter, a computer video file consists of a series of individual pictures (frames) played back rapidly to give the effect of movement. Many video compression techniques work on the basis that in any given sequence of frames there will be a large part of the frame whose contents will stay the same. For example a scene set in an indoor location may feature actors who move around, but the background of the room in which they are located will largely remain the same.

Given this general rule, many video compression techniques do not store details of each individual frame, but instead only store details of the pixels in each frame which are different to the previous frame. "Full" frames are usually stored at regular intervals, but the majority of frames are only stored in abbreviated form, capturing only the pixels which differ from the preceding frame.

This technique, coupled with the previously-discussed techniques for compressing individual frames, can enormously reduce the space required to store video content, although once again this can sometimes come at the expense of reduced quality when compared with the original uncompressed content.

Many lossy compression techniques provide options for how "lossy" the compression should be. For example, you can sometimes specify options such as "bitrates" which determine how aggressive the compression techniques will be. You may be happy with lower quality video reproduction if you will be playing back the content on a mobile phone. If you're watching it on a large high-definition TV however you will want to minimise any loss in picture quality. The trade-off is usually reduced quality in exchange for smaller file sizes.

We've looked at a few examples of how files can be compressed, but as soon as you need to use a file you will need to de-compress it. When you play back an uncompressed multimedia file the processor will be kept busy translating the content of the file into video and/or audio signals. If the file is compressed then the processor will need to do even more work to decompress it *before* it can play it back. All of this means that playing back compressed multimedia files – particularly video files – can be a very demanding process and one which can test your computer's processing capacity to the limits.

The work of compressing and decompressing multimedia files is usually done by a program called a *codec* (derived from an abbreviation of *compress* and *decompress*). Many different codecs exist, offering different methods of compressing and decompressing content. When you play back a compressed video file using a media player program that program will often require the help of a separate codec program to decompress the file. Media player programs often come with built-in codecs which handle some of the more popular compression methods. Sometimes you may come across a video file which was compressed using a codec which is not installed on your computer – in this case you will need to obtain a copy of that codec and install it on your computer before you can playback the video.

Some graphics adapters include dedicated processors for handling the decompression of video files. These processors will have one or more codecs installed. When a computer has such a graphics adapter installed, the computer's CPU will delegate the processing of video files to the graphics adapter, thus freeing itself up to do other work. This allows video files to be played back without impacting other work which is being done on the computer.

Container formats

Before video files can be read by a computer, or copied from one place to another, they need to be "packaged" in a file format that is recognised by the operating system that needs to read it. Many file formats exist for this purpose, each identified by its extension (i.e. the last part of the filename). These file formats are called *container* formats, and they define how video and audio content is stored within the file.

Container formats can be thought of as "wrappers" for the video and audio content. They do not dictate what codec is used to compress the audio or video for example, they simply tell the operating system about the content of the file - i.e. how the video, audio and other data is stored within the file. The most popular container formats are:

- 3GP – this is used by many mobile phones for video content

- AVI – this is the standard Microsoft Windows container for video content

- ASF – this is another container for Microsoft video formats

- Flash Video (FLV, F4V) – this is the video container from Adobe Systems

- Matroska (MKV) – this is a video container format which can contain a wide variety of video data

- QuickTime – this is Apple' s video container

- MPEG – this is the standard container for video compressed using the popular *MPEG-1* and *MPEG-2* codecs. MPEG-2 is commonly used on DVD disks

- MP4 - this is a container used for audio and video compressed using the *MPEG-4* codec

- Ogg – this is a container for audio and video files

- RM (RealMedia) – this is the standard container for files compressed using the RealVideo and RealAudio methods.

Copyright protection

Many files – particularly those with multimedia content - are subject to copyright protection. The copyright to a movie or commercial music release will belong to the company that produced it. In order to prevent unauthorised use or copying of copyrighted works a technology called Digital Rights Management (DRM) is often used. This technology may take a number of forms – for example some DRM systems are intended to restrict the copying of protected content. Others aim to restrict the playback or other use of copyrighted content – usually to specific users or devices.

A common DRM method is to encrypt files using a key which is specific to a particular device – e.g. a particular computer or media player. This will prevent the user from sending copies of a file to their friends, as their friends' devices will not have the key to decrypt it. The problem with this approach is that if the device in question should break in the future then the user will be unable to play back their own file on another device.

Another form of DRM is used with some broadcast media – e.g. TV shows. When the show is broadcast a "digital watermark" is also broadcast which tells digital video recorders whether or not they are allowed to record it. This method depends on the recording hardware in question being able to read this digital watermark. Sometimes digital video recorders are allowed to record the content but it can only be played back on the machine that recorded it.

DVD disks are usually protected by a DRM system called Macrovision. This prevents computer programs and DVD players from copying protected disks. Protected DVDs can also not be copied by connecting the DVD player to a VHS recorder or something similar.

Some recent forms of DRM are enforced by having messages sent to a server on the internet whenever someone attempts to access protected content. This can do things such as checking whether a user or device has permission to play back a particular file, or restricting the number of times a file is played back or copied.

High-definition video content is sometimes protected using a method called HDCP (High-bandwidth Digital Content Protection). This aims to prevent content from being copied as it travels over a connecting cable – e.g. a video cable connecting a computer to a monitor, or a Blu-Ray player to a TV set. It works by checking whether the device at the other end of the cable is authorised to play back the protected content. This device could be a TV, a computer monitor or a digital video recorder for example.

The challenge for DRM systems is to balance the need to protect the interests of copyright holders with the convenience of the people who purchase their material. This will always be difficult, as virtually any measure will place limitations on how and where copyrighted content can be used, but the ease and speed with which copyrighted content can now be shared over the internet makes this an important issue for copyright holders.

9 Mobile Devices

While the rest of this book has concerned itself with conventional computing devices, the last few years have seen mobile devices become increasingly popular. In particular, smartphones and tablets have become the preferred way of accessing email and the internet for many. This chapter provides a brief overview of the technologies available for internet-enabled mobile devices.

Evolution of mobile devices

Until the early part of the 21st century the most popular mobile device was a simple mobile telephone. Used predominantly for telephone calls, mobile internet facilities did not start to feature on these devices until the emergence of a networking technology called GPRS (General Packet Radio Service) - this provided wireless connectivity to the internet from mobile handsets. When it was first introduced at the turn of the century GPRS offered data transfer speeds comparable to dial-up internet connections. This made it useful only for a small range of purposes, and it certainly wasn't suitable for large data downloads.

Over the years this technology has evolved, with GPRS offering better data transfer speeds. A number of newer wireless network technologies are also now available, offering data transfer speeds comparable to those available to home internet users. The most common of these are often referred to as 3G or 4G - meaning 3rd generation or 4th generation networks (GPRS is regarded as a 2nd generation technology).

As internet access became more widely available for mobile handsets the handsets themselves evolved to capitalise on this. From being simple telephonic devices they soon became mobile computing devices, with miniature versions of computer operating systems built into them. The first "smartphones" appeared at the start of the century, and were an evolution of the personal digital assistant (PDA) devices which had become popular in the 1990s – thanks mostly to products such as the Palm Pilot and the Psion Organiser. Initial devices provided telephony, access to email as well as very primitive browsing of web pages. These web pages were typically restricted to those designed specifically for display on a small device.

A miniature version of Microsoft's Windows operating system was developed for use with mobile devices at the turn of the century, and began to appear on an increasing number of handsets. Over time the web browsers on these and other smartphones grew in sophistication, and were eventually able to display "normal" web pages – i.e. not just those which were designed specifically for mobile devices.

In 2007 Apple brought the first iPhone to market. This device revolutionised the smartphone market. While not offering any major functionality which was not already available on other smartphones, the iPhone set a new standard for ease of use and design styling. Its popularity effectively brought smartphones to the masses. The iPhone runs an operating system developed by Apple called IOS. This operating system only runs on Apple iPhones.

October 2008 saw the release of the first Android smartphone. Android is an operating system based on the Linux system which has been used on PCs for many years. Android was developed specifically for use on touchscreen mobile devices. Unlike IOS, Android can run on a wide range of devices. It has become the most widely used operating system on smartphones.

Most modern smartphones offer a powerful range of features which were previously only available on separate devices, for example:

- Photography
- Video recording
- Media playback (music and video)
- Satellite navigation
- Gaming
- Personal organizer (for management of diary and contacts).

Tablets

Tablets are hand-held computers which have a touchscreen but which do not require a separate keyboard. Similar to smartphones in many ways, tablets do not always offer telephone functionality but generally offer all of the other features found in smartphones, in a device which has a significantly larger screen.

The concept of tablet computers has been around for a long time. Early devices were usually designed to work in association with a stylus.

Operations were performed by "writing" or tapping with the stylus on the screen. Handwriting recognition techniques were often employed to translate the stylus movements into text. Both Apple and Microsoft introduced tablet devices in the 1990s and early 2000s, but they failed to attract interest with the general public.

In 2010 Apple finally introduced a tablet computer which found mass popularity. Called the iPad, it was a slim device with a 10-inch (diagonal) touchscreen. Like Apple smartphones, it ran Apple's IOS operating system. The tablet could be operated entirely using the touchscreen, without the need for a stylus or separate keyboard.

In 2011 the first tablet running the Android operating system was introduced. It was a similar style of device to the iPad. Since then a wide range of Android-based tablets have appeared on the market, with various screen sizes. The secondary storage of some Android devices (both smartphones and tablets) can be extended using flash memory cards similar to those used in digital cameras. This can be extremely useful if you need to store a large number of documents or multimedia files on the tablet.

The latest generation of the Microsoft Windows operating system is also now available on tablet devices, and looks virtually identical to its equivalent on desktop computers.

Apps

Much of the popularity of smartphones and tablets derives from the ability to run *apps*. Apps (short for applications) are programs which have been written specifically to run on portable devices. Apps have effectively turned smartphones and tablets into fully-fledged computers, with full internet connectivity and a huge range of programs.

Like programs on conventional computers, each app is designed to be run on a specific operating system, and will not run on other operating systems. So for example an app written for an Apple iPad or iPhone cannot be run on an Android device. Many application developers create several versions of their apps, each intended for a different mobile operating system.

The simplest way to install an app on a smartphone or tablet is to download it from the official app store for that type of hardware. For example, app stores exist for Apple, Android and Microsoft mobile devices. There is usually an app installed on the device whose purpose is to provide access to the relevant app store.

It is also possible to load apps from other sources. For example, apps may be downloaded and installed directly from websites which are unconnected to the official app store, or they may be copied onto the memory of the mobile device from another source. This practice is known as "sideloading". When obtaining apps in this way it is important to ensure that the source is trustworthy, as there is an increased risk that the app may contain malware.

By default, sideloading is usually not permitted on mobile devices. On Android devices there is an option in the device settings which allows the user to enable sideloading. On Apple devices it is not permitted at all, although it is possible for more tech-savvy users to work around this restriction by "jailbreaking" the device.

Rooting and jailbreaking mobile devices

Smartphones and tablets usually incorporate measures to prevent users tampering with the essential files required to run the device - e.g. the files used by the operating system. While this makes sense, there is an increasing desire amongst enthusiasts to expand the capabilities of their mobile device by making changes to those essential files. For example, an advanced user may want to change the style of the interface on their device to make it more attractive or to introduce more features.

There are several ways of making unauthorised changes to mobile devices for such purposes, depending on the operating system used by the device. In the case of Android the two most popular methods are:

- Rooting - enabling access to restricted system files

- Installation of custom ROMs - installing alternative versions of the Android operating system, overwriting the version which was installed when then phone was purchased.

In the case of Apple mobile devices any unauthorised change requires that the user "jailbreak" the device. This is similar in some ways to rooting an Android device, and allows access to restricted system files. Unlike Android devices, a user must jailbreak an Apple device if they want to install any software which is not officially authorised by Apple.

In the case of Android, installing software from unknown sources can be done more easily, using the "sideloading" facility described above.

As well as requiring a degree of technical expertise, the practice of jailbreaking an Apple device can be problematic. For example, installing new software updates from Apple can erase any previous jailbreaking efforts (it overwrites them).

Mobile device hardware

Like a desktop PC, the central components of a mobile device are the motherboard and the CPU. Mobile devices use miniature motherboards and specialised CPU's which are designed to minimise power consumption. They also incorporate built-in touchscreens, which allow the user to control the device without the aid of a mouse or physical keyboard. Some smartphones incorporate a small physical keyboard, either on the front of the phone, or as a slide-out panel.

Nearly all mobile devices include a wi-fi radio, allowing the device to connect to the internet when within range of a wireless router or access point. Smartphones will also have a built-in receiver for mobile telephony, which will usually allow phone calls to be made as well as connections to data networks such as GPRS and 4G to be made. Thus a smartphone will typically be able to connect to the internet in one of two ways - either via wi-fi or GPRS (or similar). Wi-fi is not usually available while on the move, so most smartphones will switch to using a data connection (e.g. GPRS) when they are not within range of a wi-fi access point or router. There is usually a cost associated with this service, which will be provided by your mobile network provider, whereas access via wi-fi is often available at no cost - e.g. at home or in the workplace.

As well as the usual computing features, today's mobile devices usually include a number of hardware options which are not considered standard for a desktop PC or laptop. Examples of these are:

- GPS (Global Positioning System) receiver - this enables the device to be aware of your geographical location, and enables services such as satellite navigation to be run

- Camera - this allows photography or video recording to be performed, as well as enabling video calling. Many mobile devices have two cameras - one on the front and one on the rear. The front-mounted camera is usually a lower quality camera than the rear camera, and is best suited for video calls.

Battery Life

One of the biggest challenges for mobile device manufacturers is battery life. The relatively small size of the devices, particularly in the case of smartphones, leaves limited space for a battery - the smaller the battery, the less charge it is capable of storing. Some smartphones mitigate this problem by having removable batteries - this allows the user to carry a spare battery which can be swapped in for the main battery if necessary.

The range of features available on the devices means that power can be drained very quickly from the battery, often requiring a recharge at least once per day. One of the most power-hungry components of a mobile device is usually the screen. For this reason it is wise not to leave the screen switched on for any longer than necessary. The radio receiver is also a major consumer of battery, particularly when connected to data networks (e.g. GPRS). This is particularly true if the device is in a weak signal area - the weaker the signal, the more battery will be consumed staying connected to it.

Some mobile devices allow additional secondary storage to be added to them, in the form of flash memory cards. These are similar to the memory cards used in digital cameras, but usually smaller in physical size to accommodate the smaller dimensions of smartphones. The most popular format for these memory cards is called Micro SD. These are roughly the size of a small fingernail, and can store data up to a capacity of 64Gb - this is enough memory to store more than 30,000 songs in MP3 format.

10 THE LAST WORD: PERFORMANCE

To close this book, we consider one of the most common concerns of a computer user: why is my computer running so slowly? In the previous chapters we mentioned a number of areas which can cause performance problems. This chapter briefly summarises the most common causes, and will hopefully give you some clues which will help you to diagnose your own problems.

The things which are most likely to make a computer run slowly are:

- Excessive disk activity
- Heavy processor usage
- Network delays.

Excessive disk activity

In an earlier chapter we explained how activities performed by a hard disk (and most other forms of secondary storage) are usually the slowest types of activity performed by computers. Hard disk activity can usually be detected by looking at the hard disk indicator light on your computer's case - if your hard disk is being used this light will flicker.

So what can cause a hard disk to be over-worked? The first thing that comes to mind is *paging* - i.e. moving data between primary storage in RAM and virtual memory on the hard disk. This happens when the computer doesn't have enough RAM to handle the programs and processes which are currently running. It needs to free up space in RAM temporarily by moving some of its contents to secondary storage (i.e. the hard disk drive), then moving it back again later. You can check whether your computer is running out of RAM using the Task Manager program in Windows, or Activity Monitor if you are using a Mac. This will show you how much of your available RAM is currently being used, and thus how likely it is that paging will be necessary. If you find that you're running out of RAM then try closing some of the programs that you have open - this should release any memory that they are using.

Another common cause of extended disk activity is virus scanning. Most anti-virus software carries out a regular scan of everything on your computer's hard disk to check for malware. While this scan is running the hard disk will be in constant use, and consequently the computer will seem to be running very slowly as any other programs will be competing with the anti-virus scan for access to the hard disk. You can mitigate this problem by scheduling the anti-virus scan to run at times when you are not using the computer.

While these are probably the two most common causes of excessive disk activity, any process which involves reading or writing large amounts of data may also cause problems. For example, copying or moving a large number of files to or from a hard disk, or searching the entire contents of your computer for a file, or something inside a file.

Another phenomenon which can cause a hard disk drive to become overworked is called *fragmentation*. To understand this we need to understand how a hard disk drive arranges data on the surface of the disk. We already know that hard disks store data magnetically, in much the same way as the cassette tapes of old. When data is stored on the surface of the disk it is divided into lots of small chunks. Each one of these chunks is called a block. Different hard disk drives may have different block sizes. For example older hard disk drives may have blocks which are 512 bytes in size, whereas a newer drive might have blocks of 4,096 bytes.

Since files are often quite large, it's often the case that a particular file occupies several blocks on the hard disk. When a large file is being written to a new, empty hard disk it will be written in a continuous set of blocks - i.e. all of the blocks in the file will be arranged alongside each other on the disk surface. When the next file is written to the disk it may be written to the next available series of blocks on the disk. This is good, as whenever the hard disk needs to read the file later it can do so without too much effort - i.e. it only needs to scan one area of the disk surface to read each entire file.

However as the disk begins to fill up problems start to arise, particularly when files are deleted from the disk. When a file is deleted the blocks that it previously occupied are released so that the hard disk can re-use them for storing new files. But what if a new file is quite large, and will not fit into the blocks which were previously occupied by the deleted file? Firstly the hard disk will try to find a large enough area on the disk surface to store the new file in its entirety. If it can't find a large enough space then it will need to fragment the new file however - i.e. store different pieces of it in different areas of the disk surface. This means that whenever the disk drive needs to read the file later it may need to scan several different areas of the disk surface to locate all of the pieces of the file. This makes the hard drive work harder, and takes more time.

The problem of fragmentation gets worse as a hard disk becomes full - i.e. there are fewer areas of the disk available to accommodate large files, and a more frequent need to break files into smaller pieces for storage in the remaining free blocks on the disk. Fortunately, programs exist which will defragment hard disks. They work by re-shuffling the contents of a hard disk to that the blocks belonging to each file are stored alongside each other. Running such a program from time can help to improve the speed of your hard disk drive.

If you regularly suffer from excessive disk usage, due to any of the above causes, you may be able to improve the situation by replacing your hard disk with a faster model, or better still with a solid state disk (SSD). There are limits to the improvements that this can bring however, so it's usually best to tackle the root cause of the problem rather than hope that faster hardware will save the day.

Heavy processor usage

While modern processors are designed to do lots of things at the same time, they can be become saturated when the workload is too heavy. Once again, the Task Manager/Activity Monitor program can tell you how hard a CPU is working. These programs will show you how busy the CPU is, showing this as a percentage, and will also show you which programs are using the CPU. If your CPU is running for long periods at 90-100% it is being overworked, and this will usually mean that your computer will run slowly.

There are many computer activities which can cause a processor to work hard. Some of the more common examples are:

- Encoding or decoding multimedia files - particularly video files

- Calculations being performed in very large spreadsheets with lots of formulae

- Plug-ins or javascript processing in web browsers

- "Bugs" or faults in programs which cause them to endlessly repeat a series of actions

- A virus or other piece if malware which is performing some sort of malicious processing

- Anti-virus software performing scans of your computer.

If a program is causing excessive processor usage it can often be very difficult to understand why. Often the only options are to wait for the program to finish, or to terminate it. If a program is repeatedly causing a problem then it could be a good idea to un-install it, or to check whether a newer version is available.

Network delays

If your computer is running slowly and there is no obvious sign of excessive disk activity or processor usage, the likeliest explanation is that delays are being introduced by networks that the computer is connected to. While delays are common on the internet, even on a local area network issues may arise which cause slowness.

If you experience slowness when using an internet resource - for example waiting for a web page to be displayed - it's likely that the delay is due to the internet rather than your computer. This could be caused by the web server which you are trying to access being exceptionally busy. Alternatively it could be caused by one or more of the network links somewhere between you and the web server being congested with data traffic - including other computers in your own house which might be uploading or downloading large files, or someone watching a high-definition video over the internet for example. There is often little you can do in this situation except wait for the server or networks to become less busy.

There is also a chance that there is a specific problem with your own connection to the internet - perhaps interference on the cables which connect your house to the local telephone exchange for example. This type of problem is best referred to your internet service provider for investigation.

With local area networks a range of problems can cause slowness. Like the internet, local networks can be subject to congestion if there is alot of data flowing between devices on the network. Wireless networks in particular can be vulnerable to this, as they cannot carry data as quickly as wired networks. So for example if there are several laptops or smartphones connecting to the same wireless access point, some perhaps watching internet video content, they may create congestion which causes slowness for everyone.

Accessing files on other computers on the network, or on network disk drives, can also be a source of slowness. The Windows operating system in particular can be quite slow when connecting to devices on a local network, sometimes causing the user to wait for several minutes while it attempts to connect to a device. This may be happening without you realising it. For example, if you regularly access files or folders over a network you might find that Windows will automatically look for those files or folders when it opens certain programs, or even while you are using those programs. This can result in a delay opening programs, or when trying to open or save files while working in a program.

Finally, if you're a Windows user there is one course of action which never fails to speed up a poorly performing computer: wiping your hard disk clean and re-installing the Windows operating system. Windows computers typically get slower as new programs are installed and used. Each new program adds files to the hard disk when it is installed, and each time a program is run it will typically create new files on your hard disk as it is working. These files accumulate over time, slowly filling up the hard disk and invariably causing the computer to slow down. A clean wipe and re-install will also get rid of any unwanted malware of course, as well as any old files which are no longer required. Of course it's vital to make a copy of any of your own files which you want to keep (e.g. documents, music, photos) before wiping your hard disk!

If this book has done a little to demystify the world of computing and the internet then it has served its purpose. Hopefully you are now better informed on the inner workings of the information technology in your home, and better equipped to understand problems when they arise.

ABOUT THE AUTHOR

Ian Manning is a former software developer, technical architect, software development project manager and IT director. His career included spells at a number of major companies over a 35 year period, including BT, JP Morgan and Digital as well as a number of smaller companies.

A technology enthusiast, Ian has built a broad and deep knowledge of Information Technology over the years, in both corporate and domestic environments. He has also retained hands-on skills in the deployment and maintenance of home computing and networking solutions.

Ian can be contacted via Twitter @ianmanning

www.ingramcontent.com/pod-product-compliance
Lightning Source LLC
Chambersburg PA
CBHW052149070326
40689CB00050B/2530